ATLAS OF ANCIENT HISTORY

ATLAS OF ANCIENT HISTORY

Michael Grant
Cartography by ARTHUR BANKS

Revised Edition

DORSET PRESS

Formerly published as *Ancient History Atlas*

This edition published by Dorset Press, a division of
Marboro Books Corp., by arrangement with the Macmillan
Publishing Company.

1983, Dorset Press

ISBN 0-88029-009-9
(Previously ISBN 0-02-545130-8)

Printed and bound in the United States of America

Preface

This is, in the first place, an atlas of the classical world – the ancient Greek and Roman world, which needs to be understood if we are to understand the world of today. To say that such an atlas could ever be a substitute for a historical survey would be an exaggeration. Nevertheless, geography is such a vital, indeed predominant, factor in ancient history – and such a difficult factor because of all the changes of names[1] – that the whole course of events often seems to mean practically nothing without maps, and without a lot of them, carefully devised.

Older classical atlases, apart from a varying degree of emphasis on physical aspects, tended to concentrate on political themes, and it is true enough that these stand in great need of maps. But the present volume attempts to cast the net wider, and to introduce economic, cultural, religious and other topics as well. There are also a number of town plans.

Modern research in archaeology and other fields has shown that the classical world cannot be grasped without some appreciation of what went before it. I have consequently started this book with a number of maps illustrating the Mediterranean world during the second millennium BC, and particularly during the period from 1700 BC onwards, when the international scene had already assumed a well-defined and complex appearance; and the story is carried onwards to offer brief illustrations of the Old Testament. At the other end of the story, the traditional terminal date of the ancient world, the year AD 476 when the last western emperor ceased to reign, is again not a very meaningful landmark, so I have carried on the tale until the reign of Justinian in the following century.

It will be clear enough what a very great deal is owed to the talent of Mr Arthur Banks for transcribing the written and spoken word into cartographic form. I am also most grateful to Mr Julian Shuckburgh for all the assistance he has rendered on behalf of the publishers, and I want to thank Miss Jane Dorner for assistance with the index. Finally, I have to acknowledge a substantial debt to existing classical atlases, German and English. And I must single out, for a special word of gratitude, the *Atlas of the Classical World* edited by A. A. M. van der Heyden and H. H. Scullard for Messrs Nelson, and *Westermanns Grosser Atlas zur Weltgeschichte* (Westermann, Braunschweig). They have both given me ideas and material for a number of maps.

MICHAEL GRANT
Gattaiola

1971

[1] Modern names are given after the ancient in the Index.

List of Maps

1

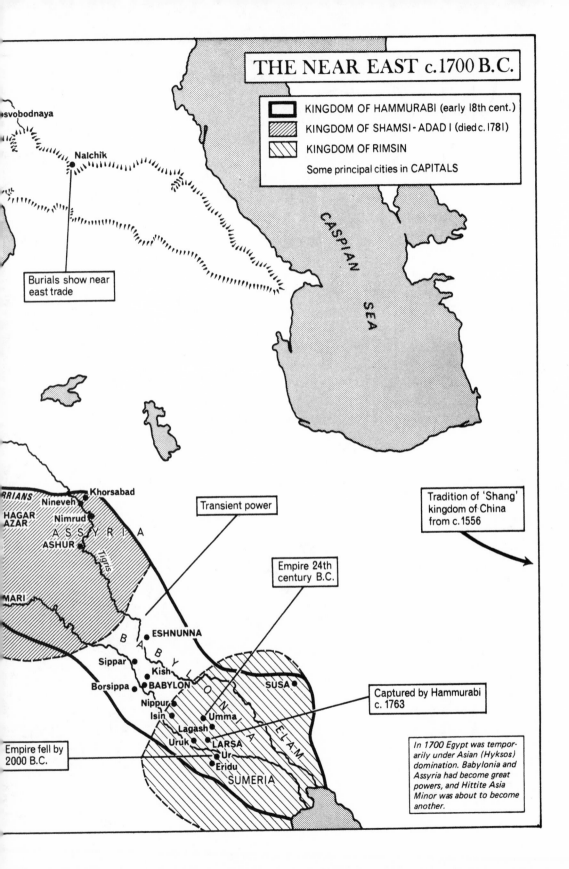

THE NEAR EAST c.1700 B.C.

□ KINGDOM OF HAMMURABI (early 18th cent.)

▨ KINGDOM OF SHAMSI - ADAD I (died c. 1781)

▨ KINGDOM OF RIMSIN

Some principal cities in CAPITALS

svobodnaya

Nalchik

CASPIAN SEA

Burials show near east trade

RRIANS

Khorsabad

Nineveh

HAGAR AZAR

Nimrud

ASSYRIA

ASHUR

Tigris

MARI

Transient power

Tradition of 'Shang' kingdom of China from c.1556

Empire 24th century B.C.

ESHNUNNA

B A B Y

Sippar

Kish

Borsippa

BABYLON

SUSA

L O N I A

ELAM

Nippur

Isin

Umma

Empire fell by 2000 B.C.

Lagash

Uruk

LARSA

Ur

Eridu

SUMERIA

Captured by Hammurabi c. 1763

In 1700 Egypt was temporarily under Asian (Hyksos) domination. Babylonia and Assyria had become great powers, and Hittite Asia Minor was about to become another.

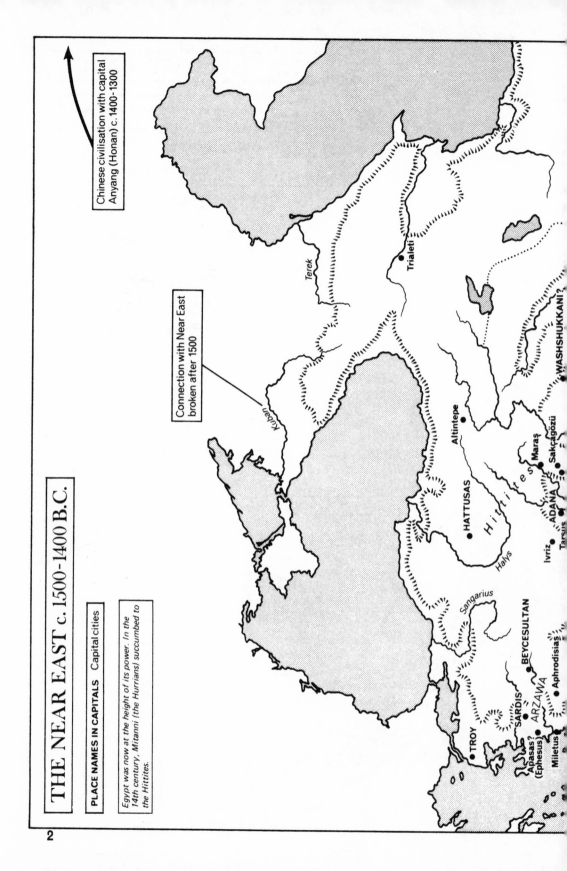

THE NEAR EAST c. 1500-1400 B.C.

PLACE NAMES IN CAPITALS Capital cities

Egypt was now at the height of its power. In the 14th century, Mitanni (the Hurrians) succumbed to the Hittites.

Chinese civilisation with capital Anyang (Honan) c. 1400-1300

Connection with Near East broken after 1500

Terek

Kuban

Trialeti

WASHSHUKKANI ?

Altintepe

Maraş

Sakçagözü

HATTUSAS

H i t t i t e s

İvriz

ADANA

Tarsus

Halys

Sangarius

BEYCESULTAN

TROY

SARDIS

ARZAWA

Apasas?
(Ephesus)

Aphrodisias

Miletus

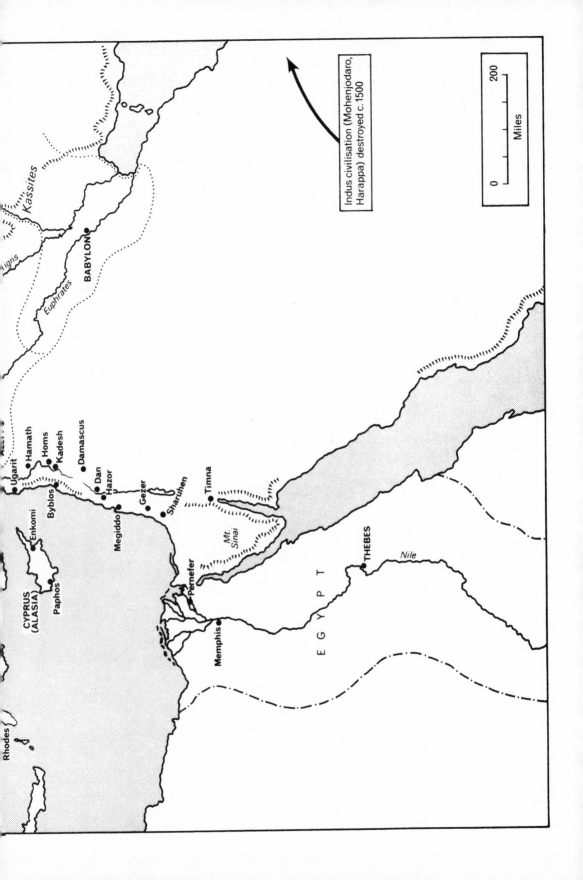

Rhodes

CYPRUS
(ALASIA)

Enkomi

Paphos

Byblos

Ugarit
Hamath
Homs
Kadesh
Damascus

Dan
Hazor

Megiddo

Gezer
Sharuhen

Timna

Mt.
Sinai

Pernefer

Memphis

E G Y P T

THEBES

Nile

BABYLON

Kassites

Tigris

Euphrates

Indus civilisation (Mohenjodaro,
Harappa) destroyed c. 1500

0   200

Miles

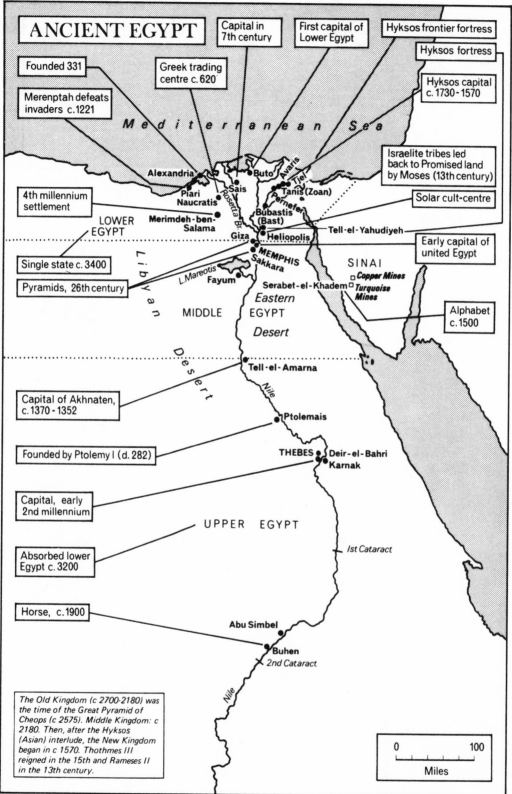

ANCIENT EGYPT

Capital in 7th century

First capital of Lower Egypt

Hyksos frontier fortress

Hyksos fortress

Greek trading centre c. 620

Hyksos capital c. 1730 - 1570

Founded 331

Merenptah defeats invaders c.1221

M e d i t e r r a n e a n   S e a

Israelite tribes led back to Promised land by Moses (13th century)

Alexandria

Buto

Avaris

Tiel

Solar cult-centre

4th millennium settlement

Piari
Naucratis

Sais

Tanis (Zoan)

LOWER
EGYPT

Merimdeh-ben-Salama

Pernefer

Bubastis (Bast)

Rosetta Br.

Tell-el-Yahudiyeh

Giza

Heliopolis

Early capital of united Egypt

Single state c. 3400

MEMPHIS
Sakkara

SINAI

L.Mareotis

□ *Copper Mines*

Pyramids, 26th century

Fayum

Serabet-el-Khadem

□ *Turquoise Mines*

*L
i
b
y
a
n*

Eastern

MIDDLE

EGYPT

Alphabet c. 1500

Desert

*D
e
s
e
r
t*

Tell-el-Amarna

Capital of Akhnaten, c. 1370 - 1352

Nile

Ptolemais

Founded by Ptolemy I (d. 282)

THEBES

Deir-el-Bahri

Karnak

Capital, early 2nd millennium

UPPER   EGYPT

Absorbed lower Egypt c. 3200

Ist Cataract

Horse, c.1900

Abu Simbel

Buhen

2nd Cataract

Nile

The Old Kingdom (c 2700-2180) was the time of the Great Pyramid of Cheops (c 2575). Middle Kingdom: c 2180. Then, after the Hyksos (Asian) interlude, the New Kingdom began in c 1570. Thothmes III reigned in the 15th and Rameses II in the 13th century.

0 _____ 100

Miles

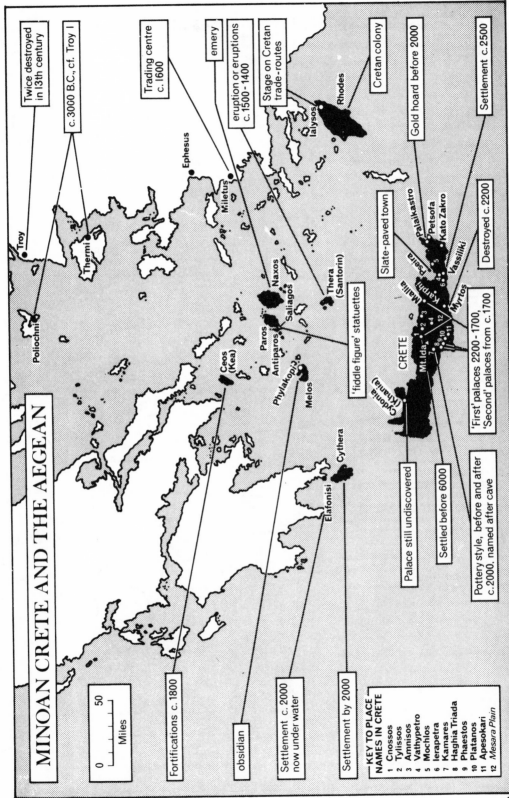

MINOAN CRETE AND THE AEGEAN

Twice destroyed in 13th century

c. 3000 B.C., cf. Troy I

emery

Trading centre c. 1600

eruption or eruptions c. 1500 - 1400

Stage on Cretan trade-routes

Cretan colony

Gold hoard before 2000

Settlement c. 2500

Destroyed c. 2200

'First' palaces 2200 - 1700, 'Second' palaces from c. 1700

Pottery style, before and after c. 2000, named after cave

Settled before 6000

Palace still undiscovered

Settlement by 2000

Settlement c. 2000 now under water

obsidian

Fortifications c. 1800

'fiddle figure' statuettes

Slate-paved town

Troy

Poliochni

Thermi

Ephesus

Miletus

Ialysos

Rhodes

Naxos

Saliagos

Thera (Santorin)

Paros

Antiparos

Ceos (Kea)

Phylakopi;b

Melos

Elafonisi

Cythera

Palaikastro

Petsofa

Kato Zakro

5

Psetra

Vassiliki

Myrtos

Mallia

Karphi

6

Mt. Ida

2 3

4

11

8 9 10 12

CRETE

Cydonia (Khania)

0 50
Miles

KEY TO PLACE
NAMES IN CRETE

1 Cnossos
2 Tylissos
3 Amnisos
4 Vathypetro
5 Mochlos
6 Ierapetra
7 Kamares
8 Haghia Triada
9 Phaestos
10 Platanos
11 Apesokari
12 *Mesara Plain*

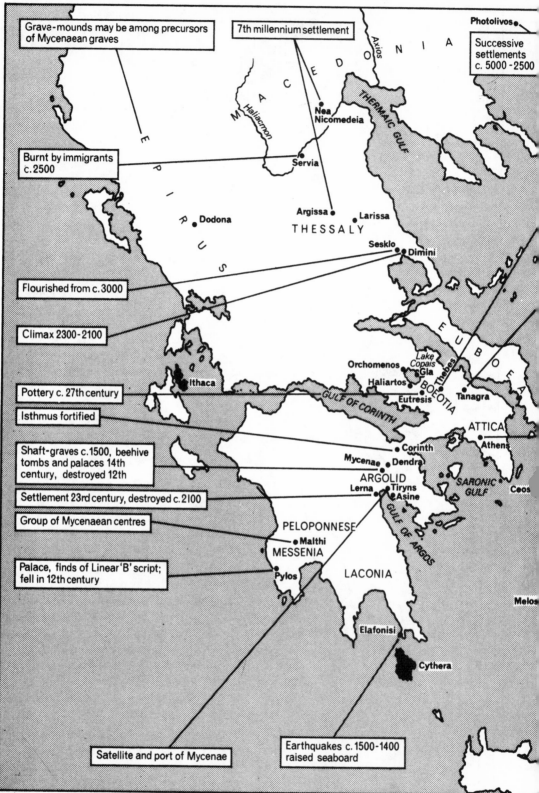

Grave-mounds may be among precursors of Mycenaean graves

7th millennium settlement

Photolivos●

Successive settlements c. 5000-2500

A X I O S

M A C E D O N I A

Haliacmon

Nea Nicomedeia

THERMAIC GULF

Burnt by immigrants c. 2500

Servia

E P I R U S

Dodona

Argissa● Larissa●

THESSALY

Sesklo●
●Dimini

Flourished from c. 3000

Climax 2300-2100

EUBOEA

Lake Copais
Orchomenos●
●Gia
Thebes
Haliartos●
BOEOTIA
Eutresis●
Tanagra●

Ithaca

Pottery c. 27th century

GULF OF CORINTH

ATTICA
Athens

Isthmus fortified

●Corinth

SARONIC GULF

Ceos

Shaft-graves c.1500, beehive tombs and palaces 14th century, destroyed 12th

Mycenae● ●Dendra

ARGOLID
Lerna● ●Tiryns
●Asine

Settlement 23rd century, destroyed c. 2100

Group of Mycenaean centres

PELOPONNESE

GULF OF ARGOS

●Malthi
MESSENIA

Palace, finds of Linear 'B' script; fell in 12th century

LACONIA

Pylos●

Melos

Elafonisi●

●Cythera

Satellite and port of Mycenae

Earthquakes c. 1500-1400 raised seaboard

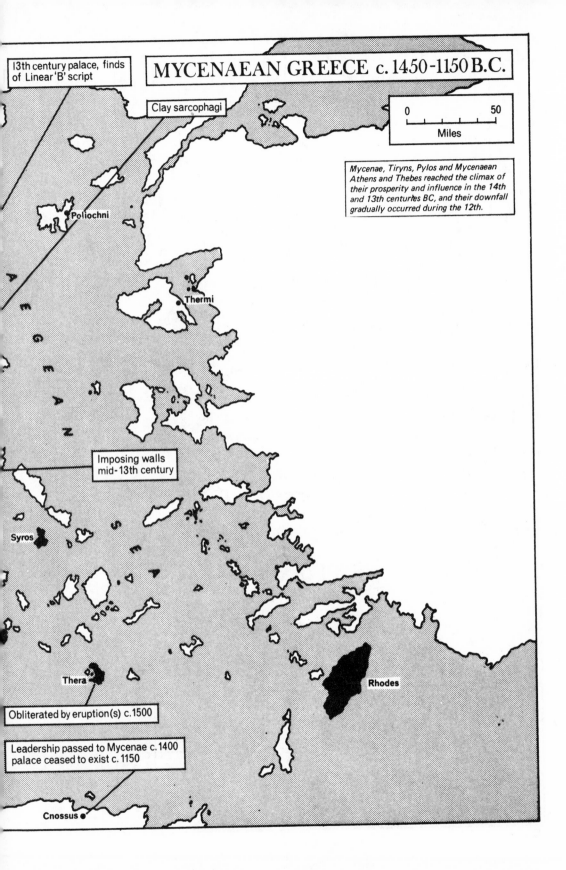

MYCENAEAN GREECE c. 1450-1150 B.C.

13th century palace, finds of Linear 'B' script

Clay sarcophagi

0   50

Miles

Mycenae, Tiryns, Pylos and Mycenaean Athens and Thebes reached the climax of their prosperity and influence in the 14th and 13th centuries BC, and their downfall gradually occurred during the 12th.

Poliochni

A E G E A N

Thermi

Imposing walls mid-13th century

S

Syros

Thera

Rhodes

Obliterated by eruption(s) c.1500

Leadership passed to Mycenae c. 1400 palace ceased to exist c. 1150

Cnossus

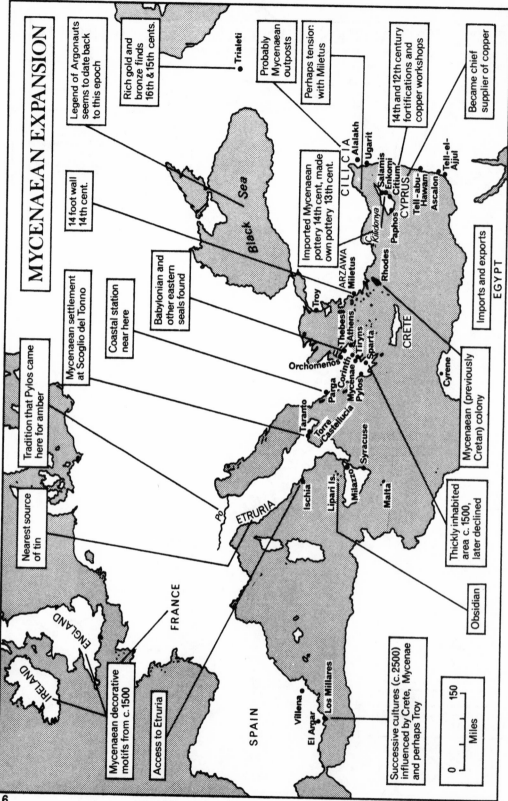

MYCENAEAN EXPANSION

Legend of Argonauts seems to date back to this epoch

Rich gold and bronze finds 16th & 15th cents.

• Trialeti

Probably Mycenaean outposts

Perhaps tension: with Miletus

14th and 12th century fortifications and copper workshops

Became chief supplier of copper

14 foot wall 14th cent.

Imported Mycenaean pottery 14th cent, made own pottery 13th cent.

CILICIA

Alalakh

Ugarit

Salamis

Enkomi

Citium

CYPRUS

Tell-abu-Hawam

Ascalon

Tell-el-Ajjul

Mycenaean settlement at Scoglio del Tonno

Coastal station near here

Babylonian and other eastern seals found

Black Sea

Kilamya

Paphos

ARZAWA

Miletus

Rhodes

Troy

EGYPT

Imports and exports

Tradition that Pylos came here for amber

Nearest source of tin

Mycenaean decorative motifs from c.1500

Access to Etruria

Po

ETRURIA

FRANCE

ENGLAND

IRELAND

SPAIN

Villena

El Argar

Los Millares

Orchomenos

Thebes

Athens

Corinth

Mycenae

Tiryns

Pylos

Sparta

CRETE

Cyrene

Parga

Taranto

Torre Castelluccia

Syracuse

Ischia

Lipari Is.

Milazzo

Malta

Mycenaean (previously Cretan) colony

Thickly inhabited area c. 1500, later declined

Obsidian

Successive cultures (c. 2500) influenced by Crete, Mycenae and perhaps Troy

0   150

Miles

6

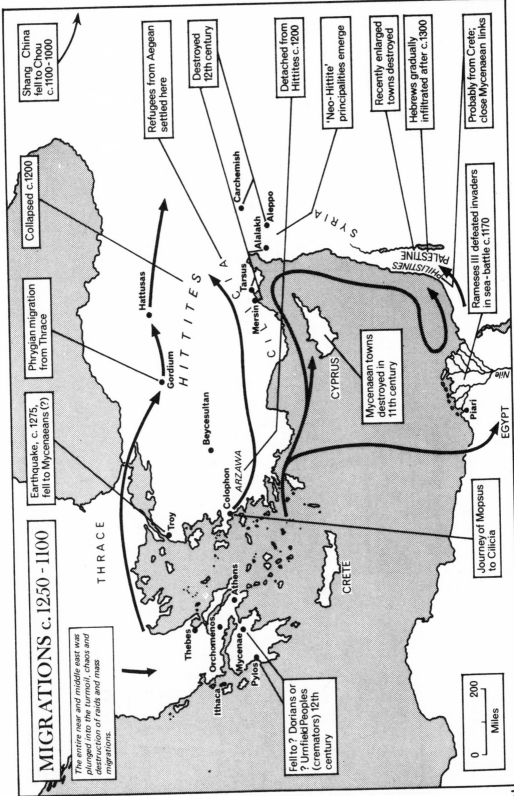

MIGRATIONS c. 1250 - 1100

The entire near and middle east was plunged into the turmoil, chaos and destruction of raids and mass migrations.

Shang China fell to Chou c. 1100-1000

Refugees from Aegean settled here

Destroyed 12th century

Detached from Hittites c. 1200

'Neo-Hittite' principalities emerge

Recently enlarged towns destroyed

Hebrews gradually infiltrated after c. 1300

Probably from Crete; close Mycenaean links

Rameses III defeated invaders in sea-battle c. 1170

Collapsed c. 1200

Phrygian migration from Thrace

Earthquake, c. 1275, fell to Mycenaeans (?)

Mycenaean towns destroyed in 11th century

Journey of Mopsus to Cilicia

Fell to ? Dorians or ? Urnfield Peoples (cremators) 12th century

THRACE

HITTITES

ARZAWA

Troy

Colophon

Beycesultan

Gordium

Hattusas

Mersin
Tarsus
Alalakh
Carchemish
Aleppo

CILICIA

SYRIA

PALESTINE
PHILISTINES

CYPRUS

CRETE

Thebes
Orchomenos
Athens
Ithaca
Mycenae
Pylos

EGYPT

Nile

Piari

0   200
Miles

7

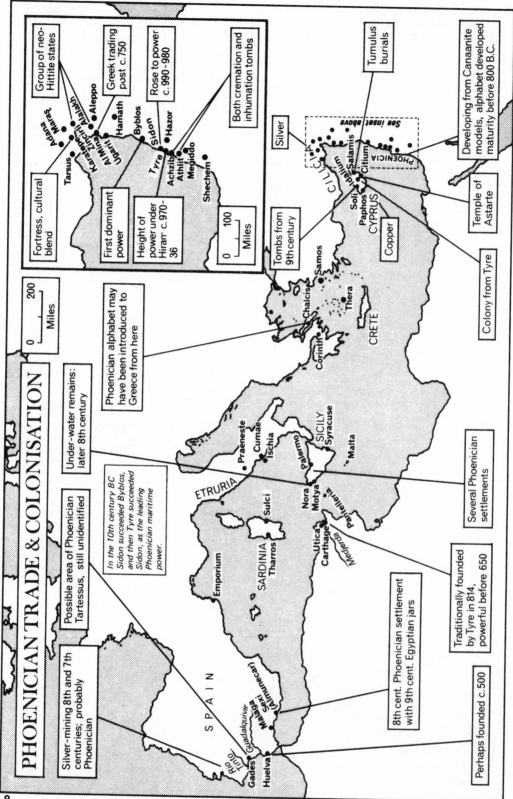

PHOENICIAN TRADE & COLONISATION

Silver-mining 8th and 7th centuries; probably Phoenician

Possible area of Phoenician Tartessus, still unidentified

Under-water remains: later 8th century

Phoenician alphabet may have been introduced to Greece from here

In the 10th century BC Sidon succeeded Byblos, and then Tyre succeeded Sidon, as the leading Phoenician maritime power.

Perhaps founded c. 500

8th cent. Phoenician settlement with 9th cent. Egyptian jars

Traditionally founded by Tyre in 814, powerful before 650

Several Phoenician settlements

Colony from Tyre

Copper

Temple of Astarte

Silver

Tumulus burials

Developing from Canaanite models, alphabet developed maturity before 800 B.C.

Tombs from 9th century

Both cremation and inhumation tombs

Height of power under Hiram c. 970–36

First dominant power

Fortress, cultural blend

Group of neo-Hittite states

Greek trading post c. 750

Rose to power c. 990–980

Place names

Arpanas, Mari
Aleppo
Tarsus
Karatepe, Alalakh
Al Mina
Ugarit
Hamath
Byblos
Sidon
Tyre
Hazor
Achzib
Athlit
Megiddo
Shechem

CILICIA
PHOENICIA
CYPRUS
Soli
Salamis
Paphos
Citium

Chalcis
Samos
Corinth
Thera
CRETE

ETRURIA
Praeneste
Cumae
Ischia
Palermo
SICILY
Syracuse
Malta
Emporium
Sardinia
Sulci
Tharros
Nora
Motya
Panormus
Utica
Carthage
Medjerda

SPAIN
Guadalquivir
Rio Tinto
Gades
Huelva
Malaga
Sexi (Almuñecar)

0 200 Miles

0 100 Miles

8

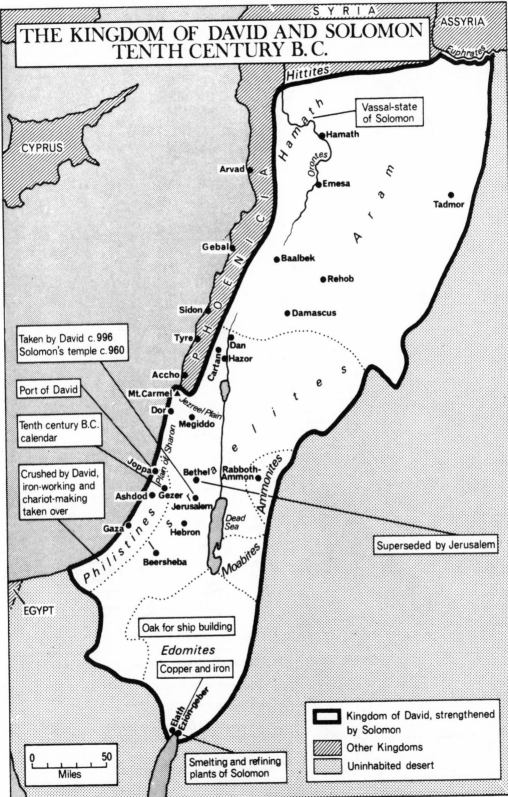

THE KINGDOM OF DAVID AND SOLOMON
TENTH CENTURY B.C.

SYRIA

ASSYRIA

Euphrates

CYPRUS

Hittites

Hamath

Vassal-state
of Solomon

●Hamath

Arvad●

Orontes

●Emesa

Tadmor●

A r a m

Gebal●

●Baalbek

●Rehob

Sidon●

●Damascus

Tyre●

●Dan

●Hazor

Cartan●

I t e s

Taken by David c.996
Solomon's temple c.960

Accho●

Mt.Carmel▲

Port of David

Dor●

Jezreel Plain

Tenth century B.C.
calendar

Megiddo●

e l l

Crushed by David,
iron-working and
chariot-making
taken over

Joppa●

Bethel◊

Rabboth-
Ammon●

Plain of Sharon

Ashdod● ●Gezer

Ammonites

Jerusalem●

Superseded by Jerusalem

Gaza●

Hebron●

*Dead
Sea*

P h i l i s t i n e s

Beersheba●

Moabites

EGYPT

Oak for ship building

Edomites

Copper and iron

Elath
Ezion-geber

0   50
Miles

Smelting and refining
plants of Solomon

□ Kingdom of David, strengthened
by Solomon

▨ Other Kingdoms

☐ Uninhabited desert

9

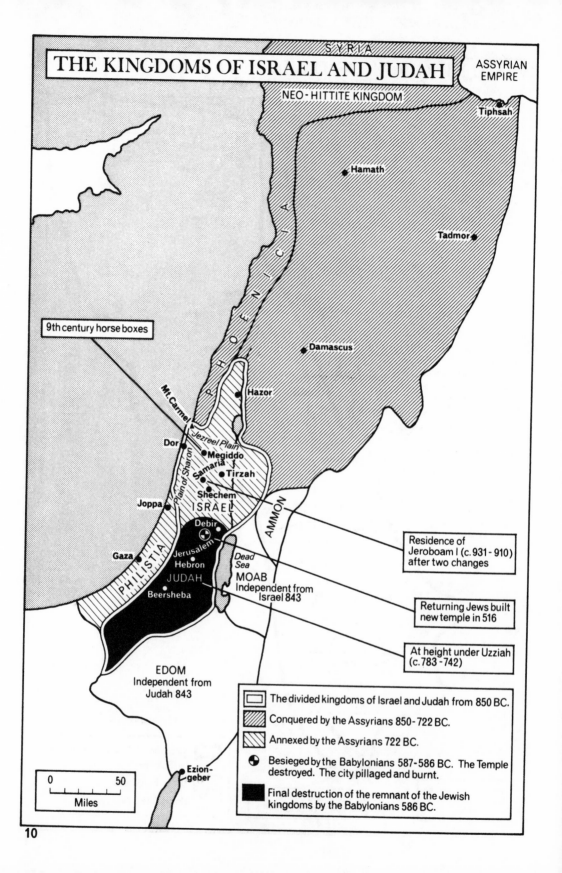

THE KINGDOMS OF ISRAEL AND JUDAH

SYRIA

NEO-HITTITE KINGDOM

ASSYRIAN EMPIRE

Tiphsah

Hamath

Tadmor

9th century horse boxes

Damascus

P H O E N I C I A

Mt. Carmel

Hazor

Jezreel Plain

Dor

Megiddo

Plain of Sharon

Samaria

Tirzah

Shechem

Joppa

ISRAEL

Debir

Gaza

Jerusalem

Hebron

Dead Sea

AMMON

Residence of Jeroboam I (c. 931 - 910) after two changes

MOAB
Independent from Israel 843

PHILISTIA

JUDAH

Beersheba

Returning Jews built new temple in 516

At height under Uzziah (c. 783 - 742)

EDOM
Independent from Judah 843

Ezion-geber

0   50
Miles

☐ The divided kingdoms of Israel and Judah from 850 BC.

▨ Conquered by the Assyrians 850-722 BC.

▨ Annexed by the Assyrians 722 BC.

✦ Besieged by the Babylonians 587-586 BC. The Temple destroyed. The city pillaged and burnt.

■ Final destruction of the remnant of the Jewish kingdoms by the Babylonians 586 BC.

10

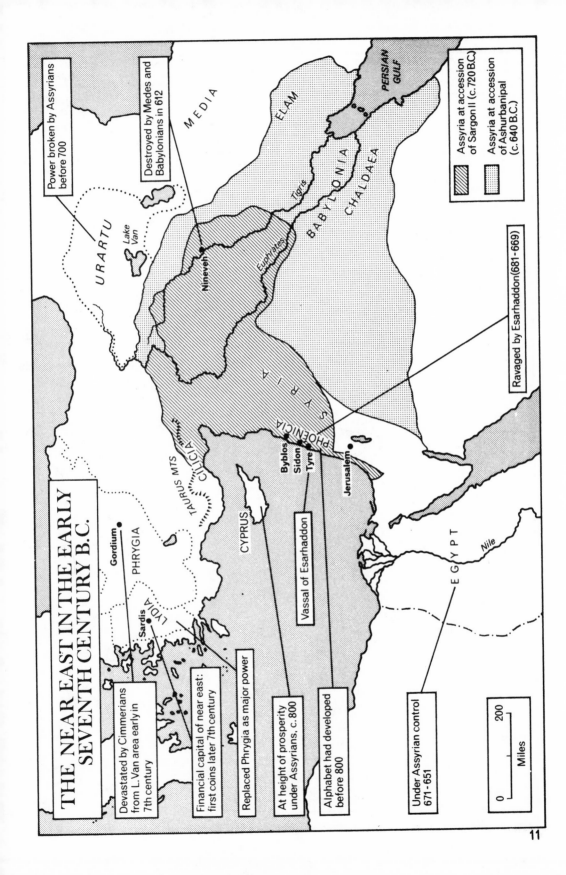

THE NEAR EAST IN THE EARLY SEVENTH CENTURY B.C.

Power broken by Assyrians before 700

Destroyed by Medes and Babylonians in 612

Assyria at accession of Sargon II (c. 720 B.C.)

Assyria at accession of Ashurbanipal (c. 640 B.C.)

Ravaged by Esarhaddon (681-669)

Devastated by Cimmerians from L. Van area early in 7th century

Financial capital of near east: first coins later 7th century

Replaced Phrygia as major power

At height of prosperity under Assyrians, c. 800

Alphabet had developed before 800

Vassal of Esarhaddon

Under Assyrian control 671-651

MEDIA

ELAM

PERSIAN GULF

URARTU

Lake Van

Nineveh

BABYLONIA

CHALDAEA

Tigris

Euphrates

SYRIA

PHOENICIA

Byblos

Sidon

Tyre

Jerusalem

CILICIA

TAURUS MTS

CYPRUS

GORDIUM Gordium

PHRYGIA

LYDIA

Sardis

EGYPT

Nile

0   200

Miles

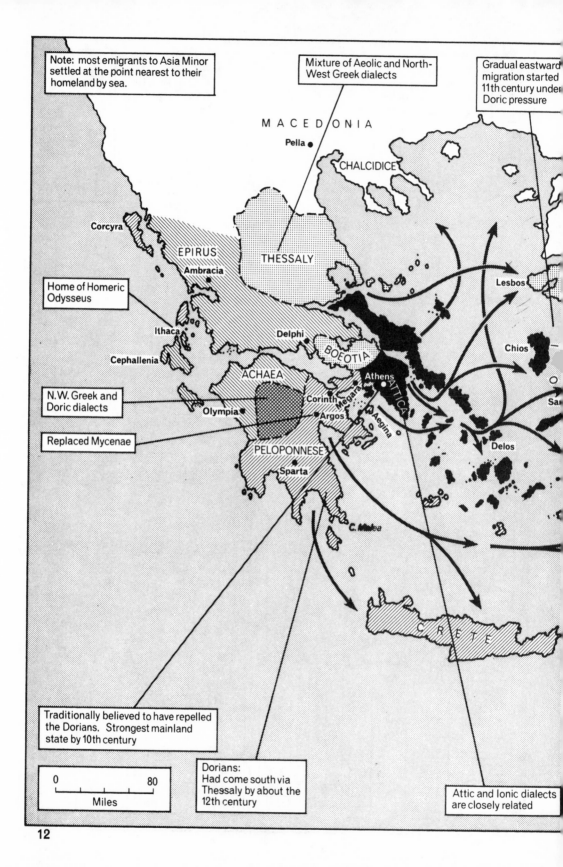

Note: most emigrants to Asia Minor settled at the point nearest to their homeland by sea.

Mixture of Aeolic and North-West Greek dialects

Gradual eastward migration started 11th century under Doric pressure

MACEDONIA

Pella

CHALCIDICE

Corcyra

EPIRUS

THESSALY

Ambracia

Lesbos

Home of Homeric Odysseus

Ithaca

Delphi

Chios

Cephallenia

BOEOTIA

ACHAEA

Athens

ATTICA

N.W. Greek and Doric dialects

Corinth

Megara

Olympia

Argos

Aegina

Delos

Replaced Mycenae

PELOPONNESE

Sparta

C. Malea

CRETE

Traditionally believed to have repelled the Dorians. Strongest mainland state by 10th century

0   80
Miles

Dorians: Had come south via Thessaly by about the 12th century

Attic and Ionic dialects are closely related

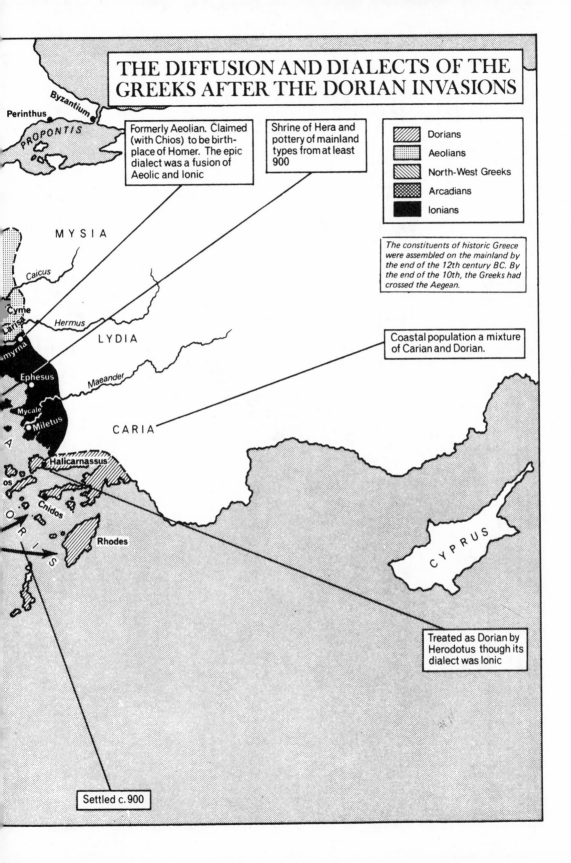

THE DIFFUSION AND DIALECTS OF THE GREEKS AFTER THE DORIAN INVASIONS

Formerly Aeolian. Claimed (with Chios) to be birth-place of Homer. The epic dialect was a fusion of Aeolic and Ionic

Shrine of Hera and pottery of mainland types from at least 900

Dorians

Aeolians

North-West Greeks

Arcadians

Ionians

The constituents of historic Greece were assembled on the mainland by the end of the 12th century BC. By the end of the 10th, the Greeks had crossed the Aegean.

Coastal population a mixture of Carian and Dorian.

Treated as Dorian by Herodotus though its dialect was Ionic

Settled c. 900

Byzantium

Perinthus

PROPONTIS

MYSIA

Caicus

Cyme

Larisa

Hermus

LYDIA

smyrna

Ephesus

Maeander

Mycale

Miletus

CARIA

Halicarnassus

os

Cnidos

D O R I S

Rhodes

CYPRUS

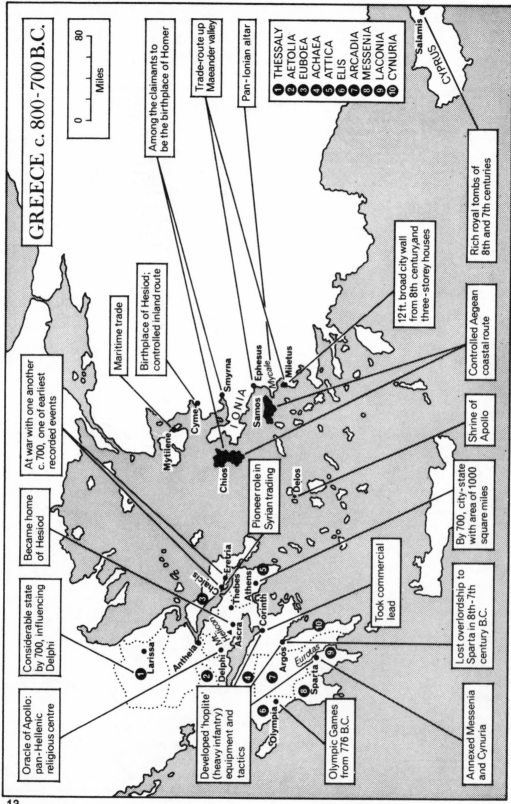

GREECE c. 800 - 700 B.C.

Miles
0 — 80

① THESSALY
② AETOLIA
③ EUBOEA
④ ACHAEA
⑤ ATTICA
⑥ ELIS
⑦ ARCADIA
⑧ MESSENIA
⑨ LACONIA
⑩ CYNURIA

Among the claimants to be the birthplace of Homer

Trade-route up Maeander valley

Pan-Ionian altar

Maritime trade

Birthplace of Hesiod; controlled inland route

At war with one another c. 700, one of earliest recorded events

Became home of Hesiod

Considerable state by 700, influencing Delphi

Oracle of Apollo: pan-Hellenic religious centre

Developed 'hoplite' (heavy infantry) equipment and tactics

Olympic Games from 776 B.C.

Annexed Messenia and Cynuria

Lost overlordship to Sparta in 8th-7th century B.C.

Took commercial lead

By 700, city-state with area of 1000 square miles

Shrine of Apollo

Controlled Aegean coastal route

Rich royal tombs of 8th and 7th centuries

12 ft. broad city wall from 8th century, and three-storey houses

Pioneer role in Syrian trading

CYPRUS

Salamis

Smyrna

Ephesus

Miletus

Mycale

Samos

Chios

IONIA

Cyme

Mytilene

Delos

Eretria

Chalcis

Thebes

Athens

Corinth

Argos

Sparta

Olympia

Eurotas

Larissa

Anthela

Delphi

Mt. Helicon

Ascra

13

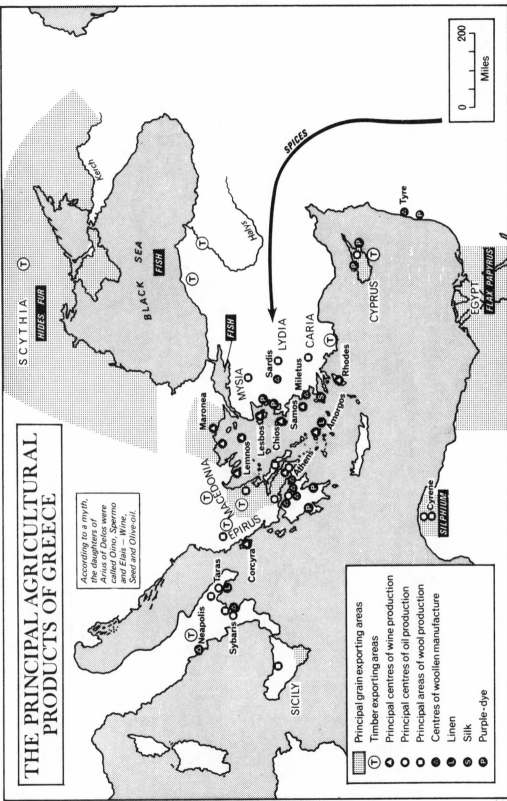

THE PRINCIPAL AGRICULTURAL PRODUCTS OF GREECE

According to a myth, the daughters of Arius of Delos were called Oino, Spermo and Elais – Wine, Seed and Olive-oil.

SCYTHIA

HIDES FUR

BLACK SEA

FISH

Kerch

Halys

T

T

FISH

SPICES

Tyre

P

P

P

T

CYPRUS

LYDIA

Sardis

CARIA

Miletus

T

Rhodes

EGYPT

FLAX PAPYRUS

MYSIA

Maronea

Lesbos

Chios

Lemnos

Samos

Amorgos

Athens

MACEDONIA

EPIRUS

Cyrene

SILPHIUM

Corcyra

Taras

Neapolis

Sybaris

SICILY

200

0

Miles

Legend:
- Principal grain exporting areas
- Principal timber exporting areas
- (T) Principal centres of wine production
- ◀ Principal centres of oil production
- ○ Principal areas of wool production
- ◁ Centres of woollen manufacture
- (L) Linen
- (S) Silk
- (P) Purple-dye

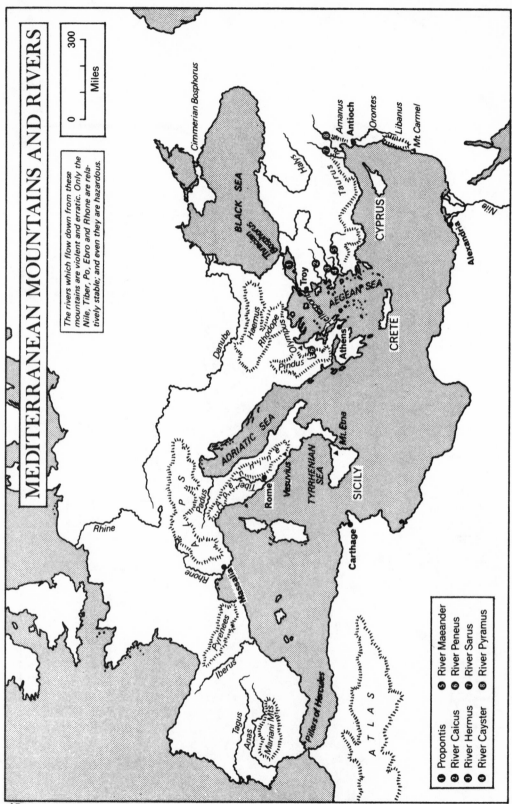

MEDITERRANEAN MOUNTAINS AND RIVERS

The rivers which flow down from these mountains are violent and erratic. Only the Nile, Tiber, Po, Ebro and Rhone are relatively stable; and even they are hazardous.

Miles
0   300

BLACK SEA

Cimmerian Bosphorus

Rhine

Danube

Haemus

Rhodope

Pindus

Olympus

Troy

AEGEAN SEA

Athens

CRETE

CYPRUS

Halys

Taurus

Amanus Antioch
Orontes
Libanus
Mt Carmel

Alexandria

Nile

ADRIATIC SEA

ALPS

Padus

Tiber

Rome

Vesuvius

TYRRHENIAN SEA

Mt. Etna

SICILY

Carthage

Massilia

Rhone

Pyrenees

Iberus

Tagus

Anas

Mariani Mts

Pillars of Hercules

ATLAS

① Propontis
② River Caicus
③ River Hermus
④ River Cayster
⑤ River Maeander
⑥ River Peneus
⑦ River Sarus
⑧ River Pyramus

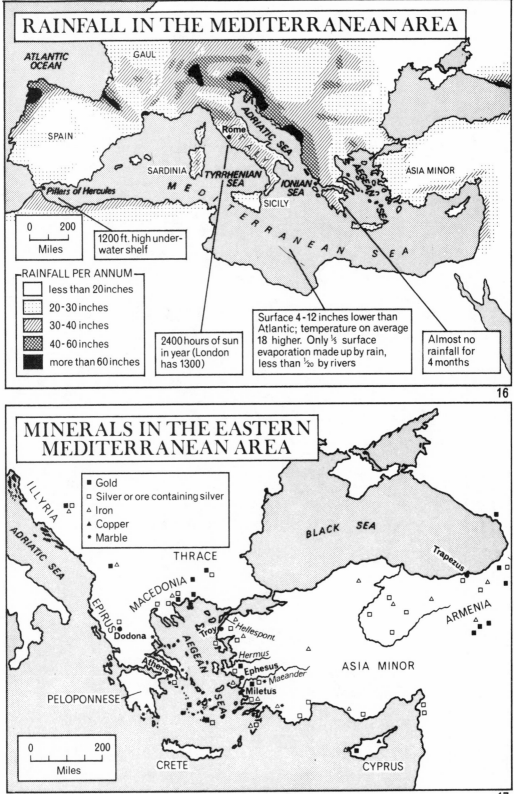

RAINFALL IN THE MEDITERRANEAN AREA

ATLANTIC OCEAN

GAUL

SPAIN

SARDINIA

Rome

ITALY

ADRIATIC SEA

ASIA MINOR

Pillars of Hercules

M E D I T E R R A N E A N   S E A

TYRRHENIAN SEA

IONIAN SEA

AEGEAN SEA

SICILY

0   200
Miles

1200 ft. high under-water shelf

RAINFALL PER ANNUM

☐ less than 20 inches
▨ 20 - 30 inches
▨ 30 - 40 inches
▨ 40 - 60 inches
■ more than 60 inches

2400 hours of sun in year (London has 1300)

Surface 4 - 12 inches lower than Atlantic; temperature on average 18 higher. Only ⅓ surface evaporation made up by rain, less than ¹⁄₂₀ by rivers

Almost no rainfall for 4 months

16

MINERALS IN THE EASTERN MEDITERRANEAN AREA

ILLYRIA

ADRIATIC SEA

BLACK SEA

Trapezus

■ Gold
☐ Silver or ore containing silver
△ Iron
▲ Copper
✦ Marble

THRACE

MACEDONIA

ARMENIA

EPIRUS

Dodona

Troy

Hellespont

Hermus

AEGEAN SEA

Ephesus

Maeander

Miletus

ASIA MINOR

Athens

PELOPONNESE

0   200
Miles

CRETE

CYPRUS

17

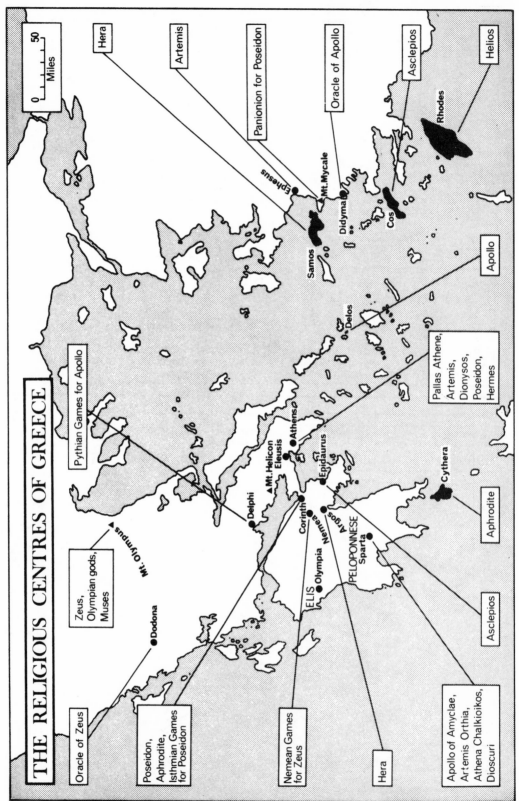

THE RELIGIOUS CENTRES OF GREECE

Oracle of Zeus

Zeus, Olympian gods, Muses

Pythian Games for Apollo

Poseidon, Aphrodite, Isthmian Games for Poseidon

Nemean Games for Zeus

Hera

Apollo of Amyclae, Artemis Orthia, Athena Chalkioikos, Dioscuri

Asclepios

Aphrodite

Hera

Pallas Athene, Artemis, Dionysos, Poseidon, Hermes

Apollo

Helios

Asclepios

Oracle of Apollo

Panionion for Poseidon

Artemis

Hera

Dodona

Mt. Olympus ▲

Delphi

Mt. Helicon ▲
Eleusis
Athens

Corinth
Nemea
Argos
Epidaurus

ELIS
Olympia

PELOPONNESE
Sparta

Cythera

Delos

Ephesus
Mt. Mycale ▲
Samos
Didyma
Cos
Rhodes

50
0   Miles

18

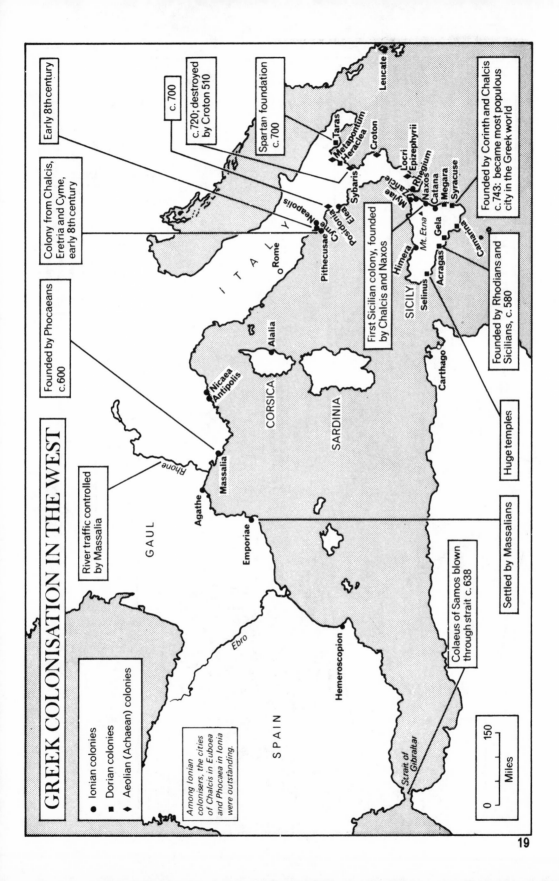

GREEK COLONISATION IN THE WEST

- ● Ionian colonies
- ■ Dorian colonies
- ◆ Aeolian (Achaean) colonies

Among Ionian colonisers, the cities of Chalcis in Euboea and Phocaea in Ionia were outstanding.

0 _____ 150

Miles

Early 8th century

c. 700

c. 720; destroyed by Croton 510

Spartan foundation c. 700

Colony from Chalcis, Eretria and Cyme, early 8th century

Founded by Corinth and Chalcis c. 743: became most populous city in the Greek world

First Sicilian colony, founded by Chalcis and Naxos

Founded by Phocaeans c. 600

Founded by Rhodians and Sicilians, c. 580

River traffic controlled by Massalia

Huge temples

Settled by Massalians

Colaeus of Samos blown through strait c. 638

Leucate

Taras
Metapontum
Heraclea
Croton
Sybaris
Locri
Epizephyrii
Rhegium
Mylae
Zancle
Naxos
Catana
Megara
Syracuse
Elea
Cyme
Posidonia
Neapolis
Pithecusae

Rome

I T A L Y

SICILY
Mt. Etna
Himera
Gela
Selinus
Acragas
Camarina

Alalia

Nicaea
Antipolis

CORSICA

SARDINIA

Massalia

Agathe

GAUL

Rhone

Emporiae

Ebro

Hemeroscopion

S P A I N

Strait of Gibraltar

Carthago

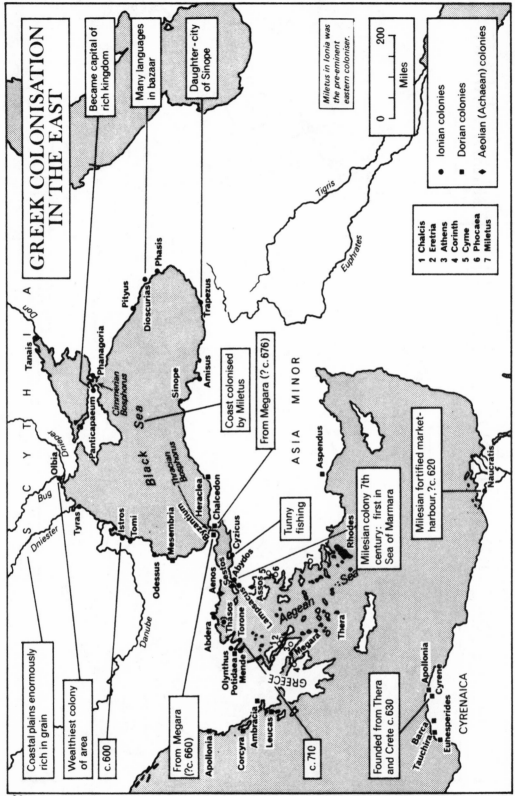

GREEK COLONISATION IN THE EAST

Miletus in Ionia was the pre-eminent eastern coloniser.

200

Miles

0

- ● Ionian colonies
- ■ Dorian colonies
- ◆ Aeolian (Achaean) colonies

1 Chalcis
2 Eretria
3 Athens
4 Corinth
5 Cyme
6 Phocaea
7 Miletus

Became capital of rich kingdom

Many languages in bazaar

Daughter-city of Sinope

Coast colonised by Miletus

From Megara (? c. 676)

Tunny fishing

Milesian colony 7th century: first in Sea of Marmara

Milesian fortified market-harbour, ? c. 620

Coastal plains enormously rich in grain

Wealthiest colony of area

c. 600

From Megara (? c. 660)

c. 710

Founded from Thera and Crete c. 630

ASIA MINOR

Tigris

Euphrates

Don

Tanais

Phanagoria

Phasis

Pityus

Dioscurias

Cimmerian Bosphorus

Panticapaeum

Black Sea

Sinope

Amisus

Trapezus

SCYTHIA

Olbia

Dnieper

Bug

Dniester

Tyras

Istros

Tomi

Odessus

Mesembria

Heraclea

Thracian Bosphorus

Byzantium

Chalcedon

Cyzicus

Abydos

Aspendus

Danube

Aenos

Sestos

Assos

Lemnos

5

6

7

Rhodes

Thasos

Abdera

Torone

Mende

Olynthus

Potidaea

Megara

Aegean Sea

Thera

GREECE

Apollonia

Corcyra

Ambracia

Leucas

Naucratis

Apollonia

Cyrene

Barca

Tauchira

Euesperides

CYRENAICA

20

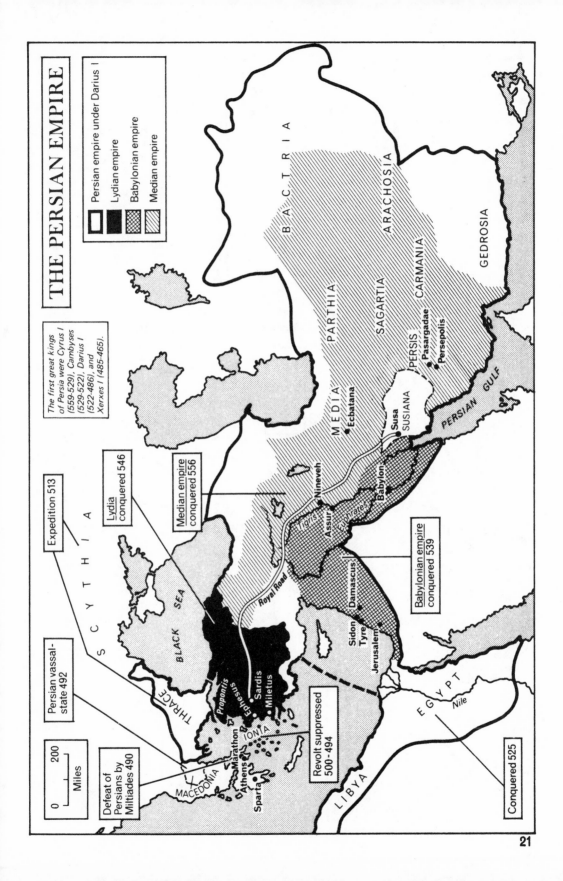

THE PERSIAN EMPIRE

Persian empire under Darius I

Lydian empire

Babylonian empire

Median empire

The first great kings of Persia were Cyrus I (559-529), Cambyses (529-521), Darius I (522-486), and Xerxes I (485-465).

Median empire conquered 556

Lydia conquered 546

Expedition 513

Persian vassal-state 492

Defeat of Persians by Miltiades 490

Revolt suppressed 500-494

Babylonian empire conquered 539

Conquered 525

BACTRIA

ARACHOSIA

GEDROSIA

PARTHIA

SAGARTIA

CARMANIA

MEDIA

PERSIS

Pasargadae

Persepolis

Ecbatana

Susa

SUSIANA

PERSIAN GULF

Nineveh

Assur

Tigris

Euphrates

Babylon

Royal Road

Damascus

Sidon

Tyre

Jerusalem

EGYPT

Nile

LIBYA

SCYTHIA

BLACK SEA

THRACE

MACEDONIA

Propontis

Ephesus

Sardis

Miletus

IONIA

Marathon

Athens

Sparta

0   200
Miles

21

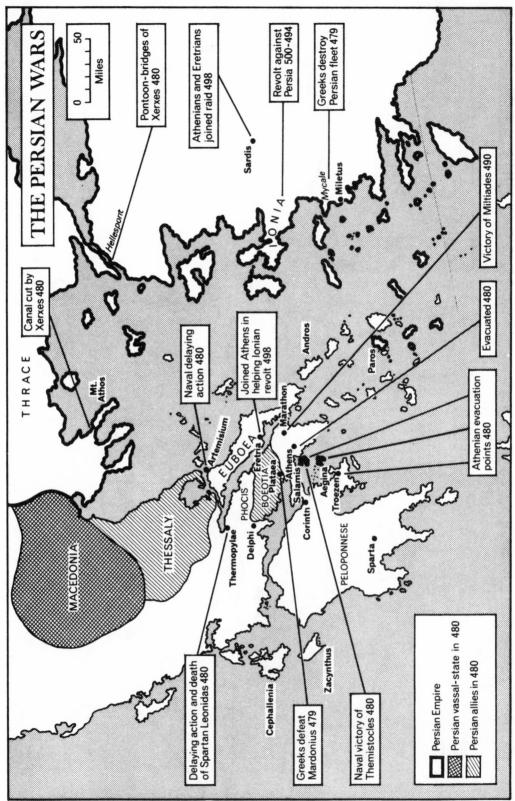

THE PERSIAN WARS

0   50

Miles

Pontoon-bridges of Xerxes 480

Athenians and Eretrians joined raid 498

Revolt against Persia 500-494

Greeks destroy Persian fleet 479

Canal cut by Xerxes 480

Naval delaying action 480

Joined Athens in helping Ionian revolt 498

Victory of Miltiades 490

Evacuated 480

Athenian evacuation points 480

Delaying action and death of Spartan Leonidas 480

Greeks defeat Mardonius 479

Naval victory of Themistocles 480

THRACE

Mt. Athos

MACEDONIA

THESSALY

PHOCIS

BOEOTIA

EUBOEA

Artemisium

Thermopylae

Delphi

Eretria

Plataea

Athens

Salamis

Marathon

Corinth

Aegina

Troezen

PELOPONNESE

Sparta

Zacynthus

Cephallenia

Hellespont

I O N I A

Sardis

Mycale

Miletus

Andros

Paros

☐ Persian Empire

▨ Persian vassal-state in 480

▧ Persian allies in 480

22

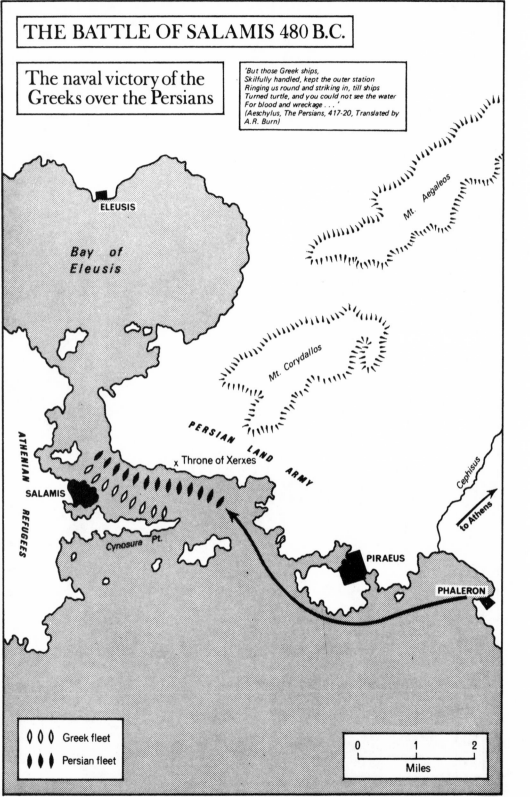

THE BATTLE OF SALAMIS 480 B.C.

The naval victory of the Greeks over the Persians

'But those Greek ships,
Skilfully handled, kept the outer station
Ringing us round and striking in, till ships
Turned turtle, and you could not see the water
For blood and wreckage . . .'
(Aeschylus, The Persians, 417-20, Translated by
A.R. Burn)

ELEUSIS

Bay of Eleusis

Mt. Aegaleos

Mt. Corydallos

PERSIAN LAND ARMY

x Throne of Xerxes

ATHENIAN REFUGEES

SALAMIS

Cynosura Pt.

PIRAEUS

Cephisus

to Athens

PHALERON

◊ ◊ ◊ Greek fleet

◆ ◆ ◆ Persian fleet

0   1   2
Miles

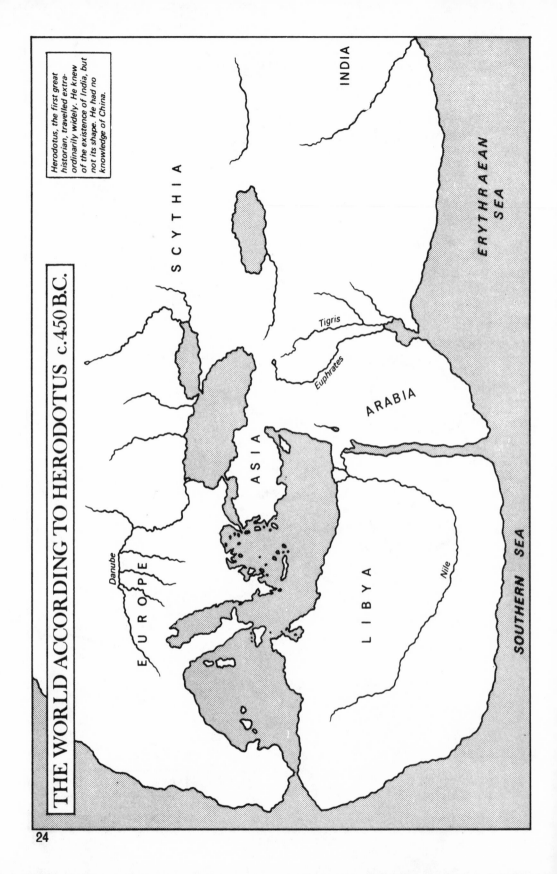

THE WORLD ACCORDING TO HERODOTUS c.450 B.C.

Herodotus, the first great historian, travelled extra-ordinarily widely. He knew of the existence of India, but not its shape. He had no knowledge of China.

INDIA

SCYTHIA

ERYTHRAEAN SEA

Tigris

Euphrates

ARABIA

ASIA

Danube

EUROPE

LIBYA

Nile

SOUTHERN SEA

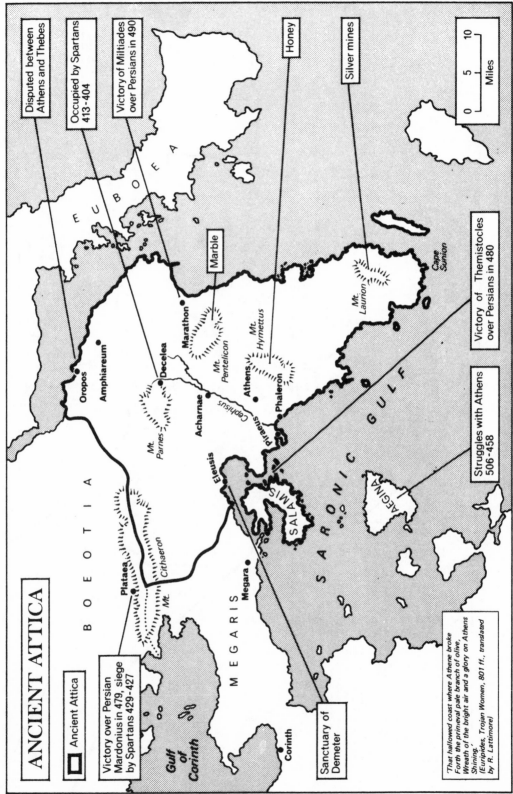

ANCIENT ATTICA

☐ Ancient Attica

Victory over Persian
Mardonius in 479, siege
by Spartans 429-427

Disputed between
Athens and Thebes

Occupied by Spartans
413-404

Victory of Miltiades
over Persians in 490

Honey

Silver mines

Marble

Victory of Themistocles
over Persians in 480

Struggles with Athens
506-458

Sanctuary of
Demeter

E U B O E A

Cape
Sunium

Mt.
Launion

Mt.
Pentelicon

Mt.
Hymettus

Marathon

Decelea

Oropos

Amphiareum

Acharnae

Athens

Phaleron

Cephisus

Piraeus

Mt.
Parnes

Eleusis

SALAMIS

A E G I N A

S A R O N I C   G U L F

B O E O T I A

Plataea

Mt.
Cithaeron

Megara

M E G A R I S

Corinth

Gulf
of
Corinth

'That hallowed coast where Athene broke
Forth the primeval pale branch of olive,
Wreath of the bright air and a glory on Athens
Shining.'
(Euripides, Trojan Women, 801 ff., translated
by R. Lattimore)

0   5   10
Miles

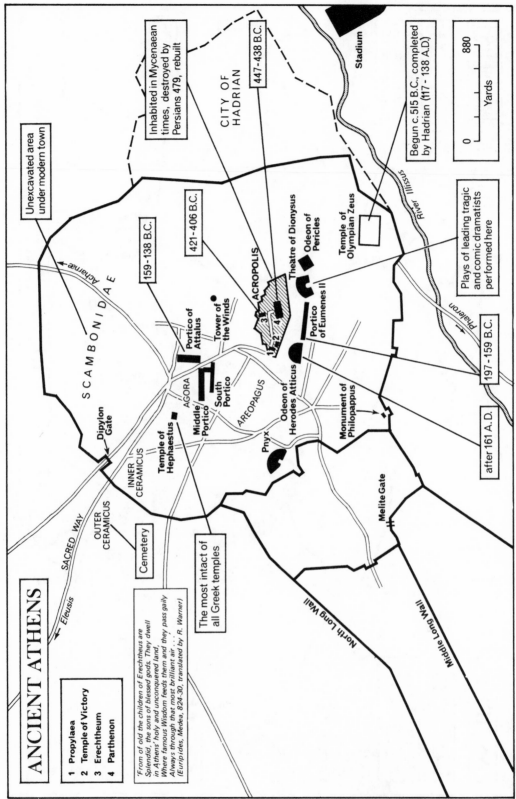

ANCIENT ATHENS

1 Propylaea
2 Temple of Victory
3 Erechtheum
4 Parthenon

"From of old the children of Erechtheus are Splendid, the sons of blessed gods. They dwell in Athens' holy and unconquered land, Where famous Wisdom feeds them and they pass gaily Always through that most brilliant air . . ." (Euripides, Medea, 824-30, translated by R. Warner)

Cemetery

The most intact of all Greek temples

Unexcavated area under modern town

Inhabited in Mycenaean times, destroyed by Persians 479, rebuilt

447-438 B.C.

159-138 B.C.

421-406 B.C.

Begun c. 515 B.C., completed by Hadrian (117-138 A.D.)

Plays of leading tragic and comic dramatists performed here

197-159 B.C.

after 161 A.D.

0   880

Yards

CITY OF HADRIAN

Stadium

ACROPOLIS

Theatre of Dionysus

Odeon of Pericles

Temple of Olympian Zeus

Portico of Eumenes II

River Illissus

Phaleron

Acharnae

S C A M B O N I D A E

Portico of Attalus

Tower of the Winds

AGORA

Middle Portico

South Portico

Temple of Hephaestus

AREOPAGUS

Pnyx

Odeon of Herodes Atticus

Monument of Philopappus

Melite Gate

Dipylon Gate

INNER CERAMICUS

OUTER CERAMICUS

SACRED WAY

Eleusis

North Long Wall

Middle Long Wall

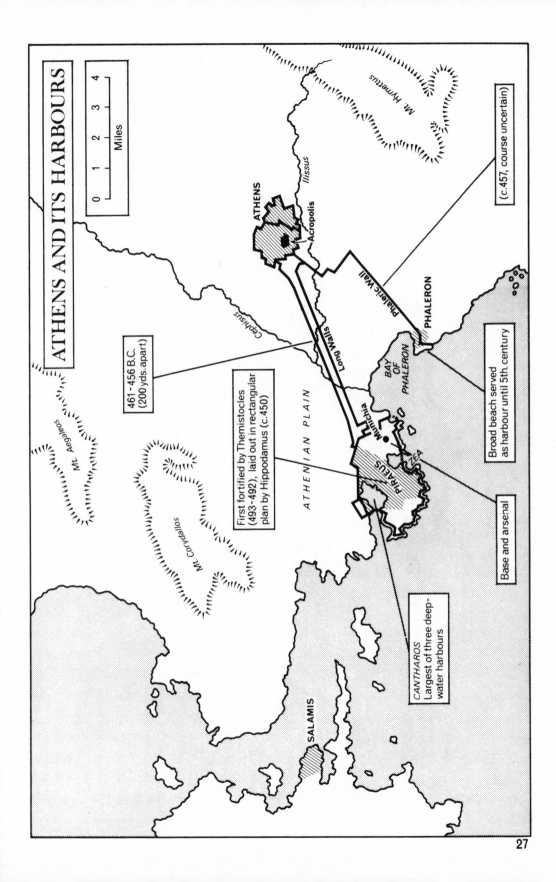

ATHENS AND ITS HARBOURS

Miles
0 1 2 3 4

Mt. Hymettus

Mt. Aegaleos

Mt. Corydallos

ATHENS

Acropolis

Ilissus

Cephisus

ATHENIAN PLAIN

Long Walls

Phaleric Wall

PHALERON

BAY OF PHALERON

Munichia

PIRAEUS

ZEA

SALAMIS

(c.457, course uncertain)

461 - 456 B.C.
(200 yds. apart)

First fortified by Themistocles
(493-492), laid out in rectangular
plan by Hippodamus (c.450)

Broad beach served
as harbour until 5th. century

Base and arsenal

CANTHAROS
Largest of three deep-
water harbours

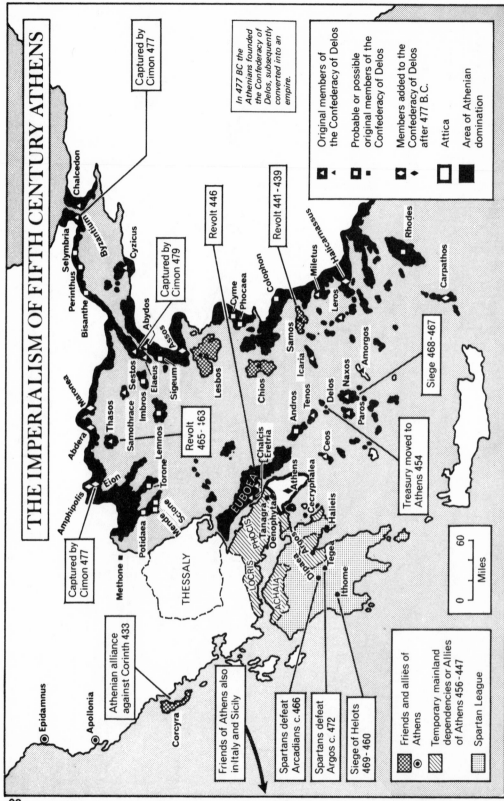

THE IMPERIALISM OF FIFTH CENTURY ATHENS

In 477 BC the Athenians founded the Confederacy of Delos, subsequently converted into an empire.

Original members of the Confederacy of Delos

Probable or possible original members of the Confederacy of Delos

Members added to the Confederacy of Delos after 477 B.C.

Attica

Area of Athenian domination

Captured by Cimon 477

Captured by Cimon 479

Revolt 446

Revolt 441-439

Revolt 465-463

Captured by Cimon 477

Siege 468-467

Treasury moved to Athens 454

Athenian alliance against Corinth 433

Friends of Athens also as in Italy and Sicily

Spartans defeat Arcadians c. 466

Spartans defeat Argos c. 472

Siege of Helots 469-460

Friends and allies of Athens

Temporary mainland dependencies or Allies of Athens 456-447

Spartan League

Chalcedon
Selymbria
Byzantium
Perinthus
Bisanthe
Cyzicus
Abydos
Asos
Sestos
Samothrace
Imbros
Elaeus
Sigeum
Maroneea
Abdera
Thasos
Lemnos
Torone
Scione
Mende
Potidaea
Amphipolis
Eion
Methone

Cyme
Phocaea
Colophon
Miletus
Halicarnassus
Rhodes
Carpathos
Samos
Icaria
Leros
Amorgos
Naxos
Paros
Delos
Tenos
Andros
Ceos
Lesbos
Chios

THESSALY
LOCRIS
PHOCIS
Tanagra
Oenophyta
Chalcis
Eretria
EUBOEA
Athens
Cecryphalea
Halieis
ACHAIA
Oenoea
Argos
Cleonae
Tegea
Ithome

Epidamnus
Apollonia
Corcyra

0   60
Miles

28

GREECE IN THE PELOPONNESIAN WAR 431-404 B.C.

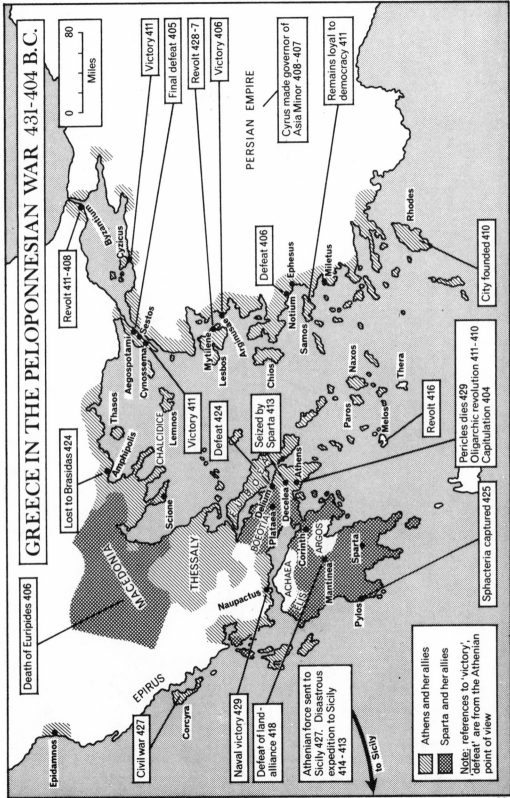

PERSIAN EMPIRE

Cyrus made governor of Asia Minor 408-407

Remains loyal to democracy 411

Victory 411

Final defeat 405

Revolt 428-7

Victory 406

Defeat 406

Rhodes

City founded 410

Revolt 411-408

Byzantium

Cyzicus

Aegospotami

Sestos

Cynossema

Notium

Ephesus

Miletus

Mytilene

Arginusae

Lesbos

Samos

Chios

Naxos

Paros

Thera

Melos

Revolt 416

Pericles dies 429
Oligarchic revolution 411-410
Capitulation 404

Thasos

Lost to Brasidas 424

Amphipolis

CHALCIDICE

Lemnos

Victory 411

Defeat 424

Seized by Sparta 413

Scione

MACEDONIA

Death of Euripides 406

THESSALY

BOEOTIA

EUBOEA

Delium

Plataea

Decelea

Athens

Corinth

ARGOS

Sparta

Mantinea

Pylos

ACHAEA
ELIS

Naupactus

Sphacteria captured 425

EPIRUS

Corcyra

Civil war 427

Naval victory 429

Defeat of land-alliance 418

Athenian force sent to Sicily 427. Disastrous expedition to Sicily 414-413

to Sicily

Epidamnos

0   80

Miles

Athens and her allies

Sparta and her allies

Note: references to 'victory',
'defeat' are from the Athenian
point of view

29

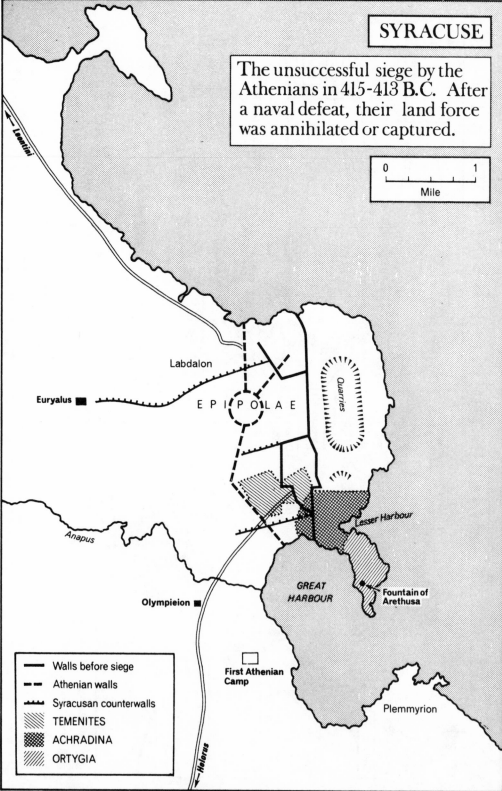

SYRACUSE

The unsuccessful siege by the Athenians in 415-413 B.C. After a naval defeat, their land force was annihilated or captured.

0 1
Mile

Leontini

Labdalon

Euryalus ■

E P I P O L A E

Quarries

Anapus

Lesser Harbour

Olympieion ■

GREAT HARBOUR

Fountain of Arethusa

First Athenian Camp

Plemmyrion

Helorus

Walls before siege
Athenian walls
Syracusan counterwalls
TEMENITES
ACHRADINA
ORTYGIA

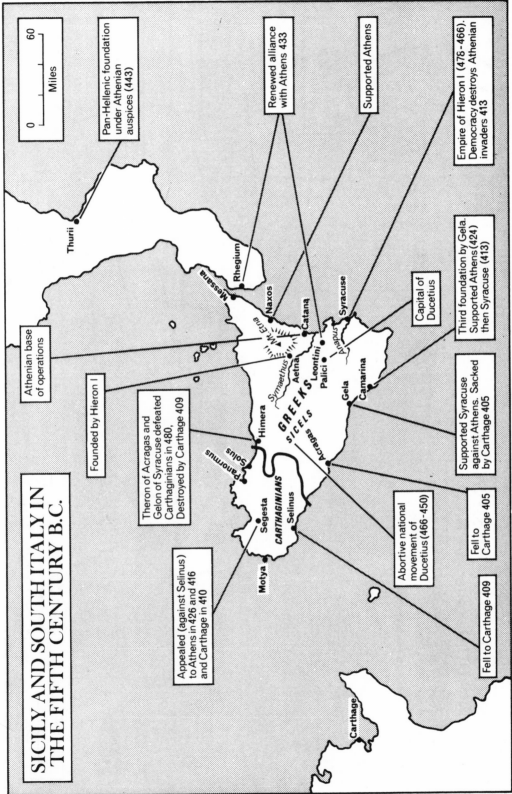

SICILY AND SOUTH ITALY IN THE FIFTH CENTURY B.C.

Pan-Hellenic foundation under Athenian auspices (443)

Renewed alliance with Athens 433

Supported Athens

Empire of Hieron I (478-466). Democracy destroys Athenian invaders 413

Athenian base of operations

Founded by Hieron I

Theron of Acragas and Gelon of Syracuse defeated Carthaginians in 480, Destroyed by Carthage 409

Appealed (against Selinus) to Athens in 426 and 416 and Carthage in 410

Capital of Ducetius

Third foundation by Gela. Supported Athens (424) then Syracuse (413)

Supported Syracuse against Athens. Sacked by Carthage 405

Abortive national movement of Ducetius (466-450)

Fell to Carthage 405

Fell to Carthage 409

Thurii

Rhegium

Messana

Naxos

Catana

Leontini

Palici

Syracuse

Mt. Etna

Aetna

Symaethus

Anapus

GREEKS

SICELS

Gela

Camarina

Himera

Solus

Panormus

Segesta

Selinus

Acragas

CARTHAGINIANS

Motya

Carthage

Miles

0   60

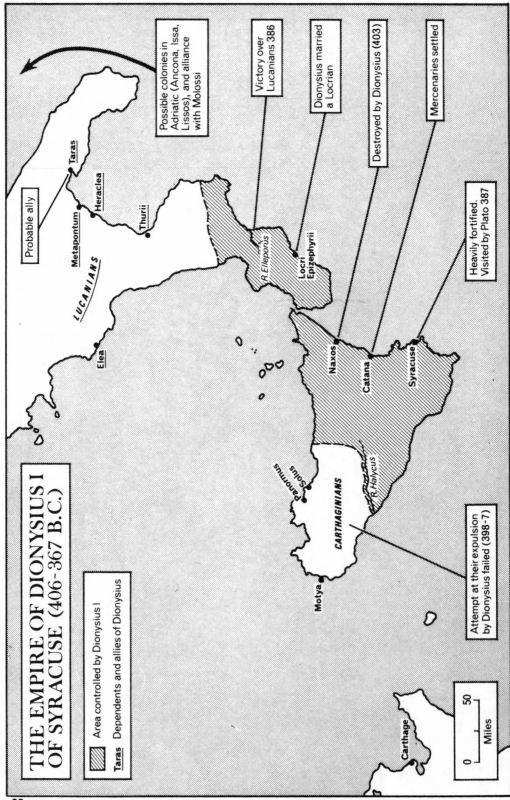

THE EMPIRE OF DIONYSIUS I OF SYRACUSE (406-367 B.C.)

Area controlled by Dionysius I

Taras Dependents and allies of Dionysius

Possible colonies in Adriatic (Ancona, Issa, Lissos), and alliance with Molossi

Victory over Lucanians 386

Dionysius married a Locrian

Destroyed by Dionysius (403)

Mercenaries settled

Heavily fortified. Visited by Plato 387

Probable ally

Taras

Heraclea

Metapontum

Thurii

LUCANIANS

Elea

R. Elleporus

Locri Epizephyrii

Naxos

Catana

Syracuse

Panormus

Solus

R. Halycus

CARTHAGINIANS

Motya

Attempt at their expulsion by Dionysius failed (398-7)

Carthage

0 50

Miles

32

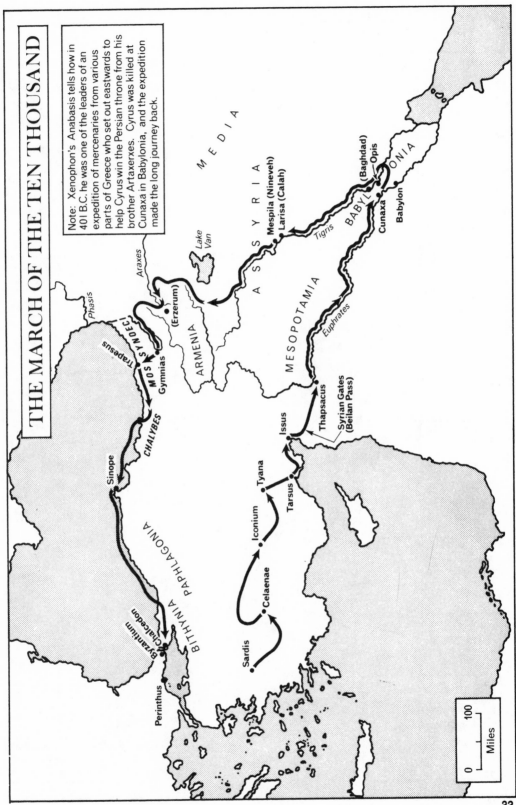

THE MARCH OF THE TEN THOUSAND

Note: Xenophon's Anabasis tells how in 401 B.C. he was one of the leaders of an expedition of mercenaries from various parts of Greece who set out eastwards to help Cyrus win the Persian throne from his brother Artaxerxes. Cyrus was killed at Cunaxa in Babylonia, and the expedition made the long journey back.

MEDIA

ASSYRIA

Mespila (Nineveh)
Larisa (Calah)

Tigris

BABY
LONIA

(Baghdad)
Opis
Cunaxa
Babylon

Araxes

Lake
Van

(Erzerum)

ARMENIA

MESOPOTAMIA

Euphrates

Phasis

Trapesus

MOS SYNOECI

Gymnias

CHALYBES

Thapsacus

Syrian Gates
(Beilan Pass)

Issus

Sinope

Tyana

Iconium

Tarsus

PAPHLAGONIA

Celaenae

BITHYNIA

Sardis

Byzantium
Chalcedon

Perinthus

0	100
Miles	

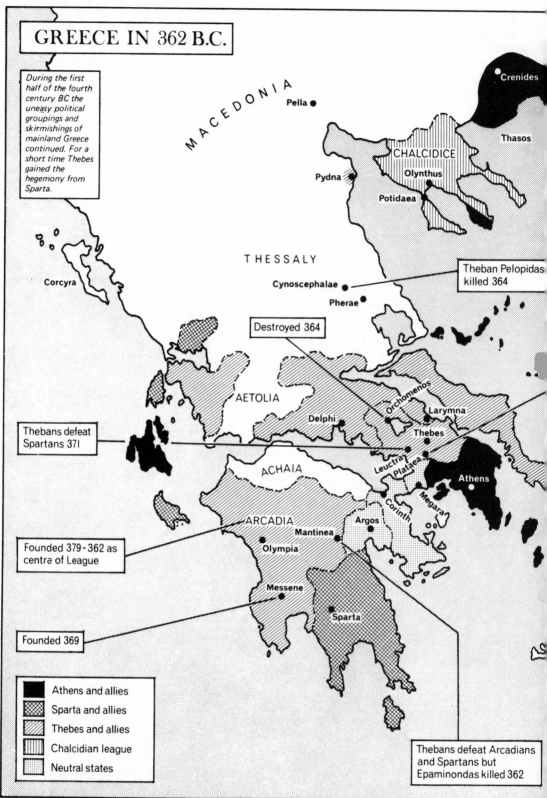

GREECE IN 362 B.C.

During the first half of the fourth century BC the uneasy political groupings and skirmishings of mainland Greece continued. For a short time Thebes gained the hegemony from Sparta.

MACEDONIA

Pella

Crenides

Thasos

CHALCIDICE

Olynthus

Pydna

Potidaea

THESSALY

Corcyra

Theban Pelopidas killed 364

Cynoscephalae

Pherae

Destroyed 364

AETOLIA

Orchomenos

Larymna

Delphi

Thebes

Thebans defeat Spartans 371

ACHAIA

Leuctra

Plataea

Athens

Megara

Corinth

ARCADIA

Argos

Founded 379-362 as centre of League

Mantinea

Olympia

Messene

Founded 369

Sparta

	Athens and allies
	Sparta and allies
	Thebes and allies
	Chalcidian league
	Neutral states

Thebans defeat Arcadians and Spartans but Epaminondas killed 362

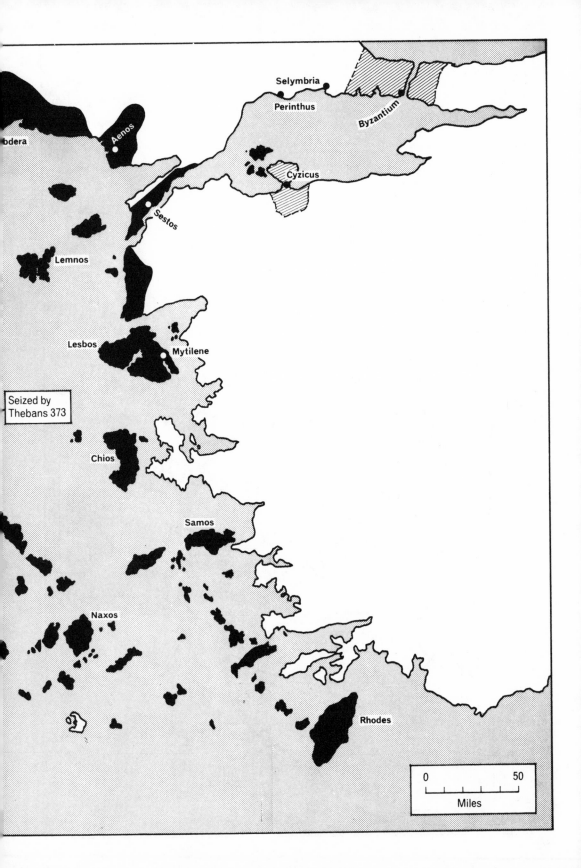

Selymbria

Perinthus

Byzantium

bdera

Aenos

Cyzicus

Sestos

Lemnos

Lesbos

Mytilene

Seized by
Thebans 373

Chios

Samos

Naxos

Rhodes

0   50

Miles

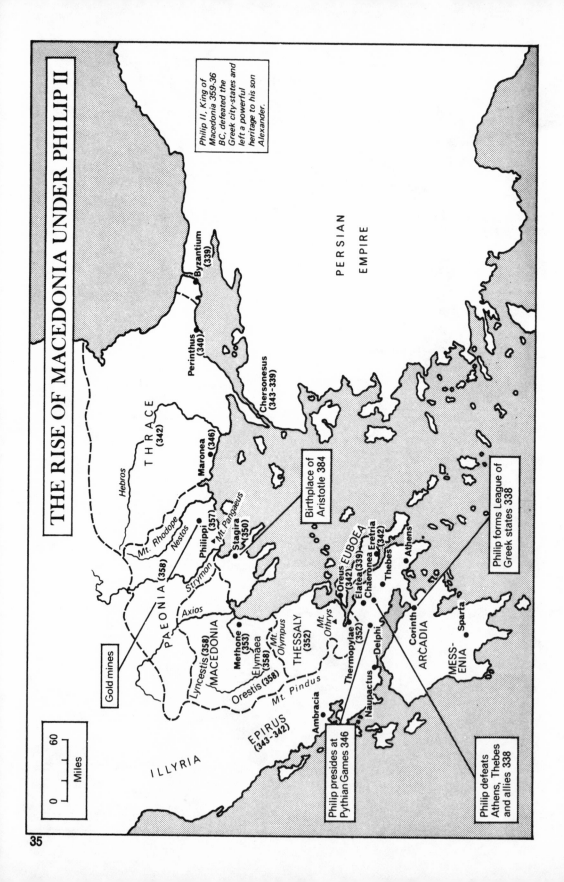

THE RISE OF MACEDONIA UNDER PHILIP II

Philip II, King of Macedonia 359-36 BC, defeated the Greek city-states and left a powerful heritage to his son Alexander.

PERSIAN EMPIRE

Byzantium (339)

Perinthus (340)

Chersonesus (343-339)

THRACE (342)

Maronea (346)

Hebros

Mt. Rhodope

Nestos

Philippi (357)

Mt. Pangaeus

Stagira (350)

Birthplace of Aristotle 384

PAEONIA (358)

Strymon

Axios

MACEDONIA

Lyncestis (358)

Methone (353)

Elymaea (358)

Orestis (358)

Mt. Olympus

THESSALY (352)

Mt. Othrys

EUBOEA

Oreus (342)

Elatea (339)

Chaeronea

Eretria (342)

Thebes

Athens

Gold mines

Philip forms League of Greek states 338

Mt. Pindus

Thermopylae (352)

Delphi

Naupactus

Corinth

ARCADIA

MESS-ENIA

Sparta

Ambracia

EPIRUS (343-342)

ILLYRIA

Philip presides at Pythian Games 346

Philip defeats Athens, Thebes and allies 338

0   60
Miles

35

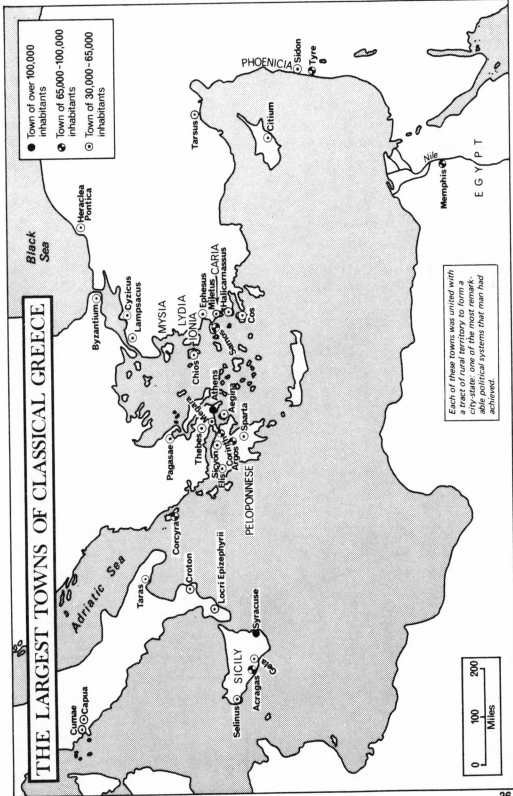

THE LARGEST TOWNS OF CLASSICAL GREECE

Legend:
- ● Town of over 100,000 inhabitants
- ◕ Town of 65,000 - 100,000 inhabitants
- ◉ Town of 30,000 - 65,000 inhabitants

Each of these towns was united with a tract of rural territory to form a city-state: one of the most remarkable political systems that man had achieved.

PHOENICIA
Sidon
Tyre
Tarsus
Citium
Nile
EGYPT
Memphis

Black Sea
Heraclea Pontica
Byzantium
Cyzicus
Lampsacus
MYSIA
LYDIA
IONIA
CARIA
Ephesus
Miletus
Halicarnassus
Cos
Chios
Samos
Athens
Megara
Aegina
Sparta
Thebes
Sicyon
Corinth
Elis
Argos
Pagasae
PELOPONNESE

Adriatic Sea
Corcyra
Taras
Croton
Locri Epizephyrii
Syracuse
Gela
SICILY
Acragas
Selinus
Cumae
Capua

0 100 200
Miles

36

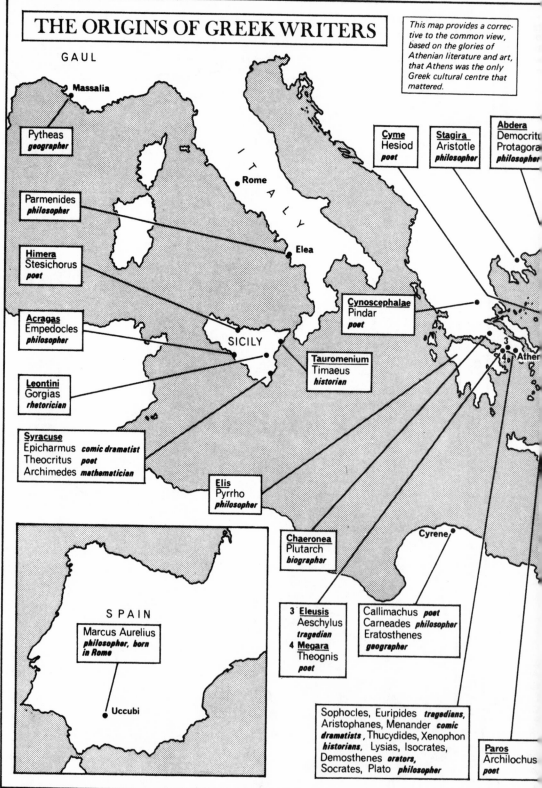

THE ORIGINS OF GREEK WRITERS

This map provides a corrective to the common view, based on the glories of Athenian literature and art, that Athens was the only Greek cultural centre that mattered.

GAUL

Massalia

Pytheas *geographer*

Parmenides *philosopher*

Himera Stesichorus *poet*

Acragas Empedocles *philosopher*

Leontini Gorgias *rhetorician*

Syracuse Epicharmus *comic dramatist* Theocritus *poet* Archimedes *mathematician*

Rome

ITALY

Elea

SICILY

Tauromenium Timaeus *historian*

Cyme Hesiod *poet*

Stagira Aristotle *philosopher*

Abdera Democritu Protagora *philosopher*

Cynoscephalae Pindar *poet*

Ather

Elis Pyrrho *philosopher*

Chaeronea Plutarch *biographer*

Cyrene

SPAIN

Marcus Aurelius *philosopher, born in Rome*

Uccubi

3 **Eleusis** Aeschylus *tragedian*
4 **Megara** Theognis *poet*

Callimachus *poet* Carneades *philosopher* Eratosthenes *geographer*

Sophocles, Euripides *tragedians,* Aristophanes, Menander *comic dramatists,* Thucydides, Xenophon *historians,* Lysias, Isocrates, Demosthenes *orators,* Socrates, Plato *philosopher*

Paros Archilochus *poet*

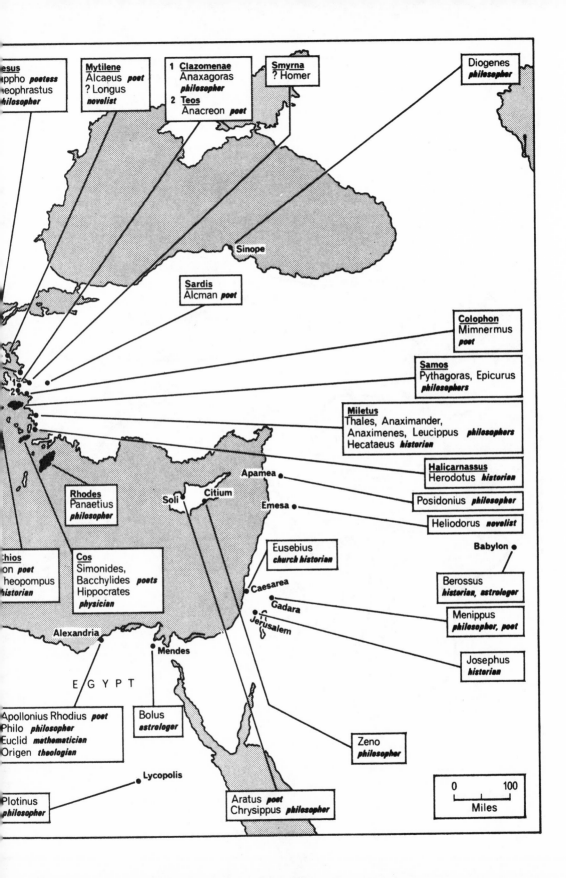

esus
appho *poetess*
heophrastus
hilosopher

Mytilene
Alcaeus *poet*
? Longus *novelist*

1 **Clazomenae**
Anaxagoras
philosopher
2 **Teos**
Anacreon *poet*

Smyrna
? Homer

Diogenes
philosopher

Sinope

Sardis
Alcman *poet*

Colophon
Mimnermus
poet

Samos
Pythagoras, Epicurus
philosophers

Miletus
Thales, Anaximander,
Anaximenes, Leucippus *philosophers*
Hecataeus *historian*

Apamea

Halicarnassus
Herodotus *historian*

Posidonius *philosopher*

Emesa

Heliodorus *novelist*

Rhodes
Panaetius
philosopher

Soli **Citium**

Babylon

Berossus
historian, astrologer

hios
on *poet*
heopompus
historian

Cos
Simonides,
Bacchylides *poets*
Hippocrates
physician

Eusebius
church historian

Caesarea

Gadara

Jerusalem

Menippus
philosopher, poet

Josephus
historian

Alexandria

Mendes

E G Y P T

Apollonius Rhodius *poet*
Philo *philosopher*
Euclid *mathematician*
Origen *theologian*

Bolus
astrologer

Zeno
philosopher

Lycopolis

Plotinus
philosopher

Aratus *poet*
Chrysippus *philosopher*

0   100

Miles

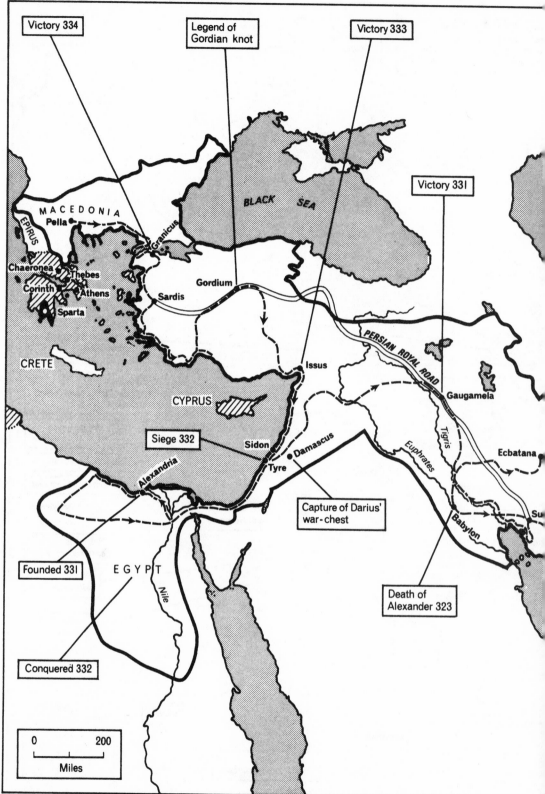

Victory 334

Legend of
Gordian knot

Victory 333

Victory 331

MACEDONIA

EPIRUS

Pella

BLACK SEA

Chaeronea

Thebes

Corinth

Athens

Sardis

Gordium

CRETE

Sparta

Issus

PERSIAN ROYAL ROAD

Gaugamela

CYPRUS

Ecbatana

Siege 332

Sidon

Damascus

Tyre

Euphrates

Tigris

Alexandria

Capture of Darius'
war-chest

Babylon

Su

Founded 331

E G Y P T

Nile

Death of
Alexander 323

Conquered 332

0   200

Miles

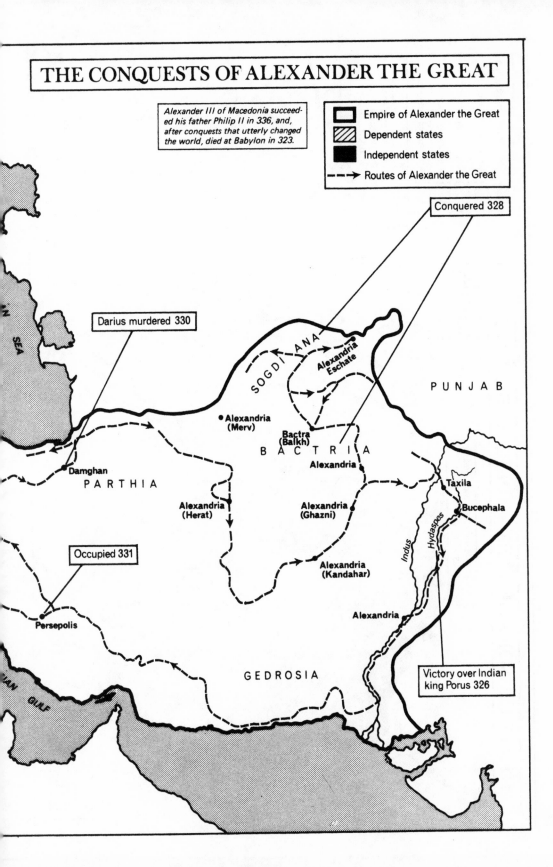

THE CONQUESTS OF ALEXANDER THE GREAT

Alexander III of Macedonia succeeded his father Philip II in 336, and, after conquests that utterly changed the world, died at Babylon in 323.

	Empire of Alexander the Great
	Dependent states
	Independent states
------>	Routes of Alexander the Great

Conquered 328

Darius murdered 330

CASPIAN SEA

SOGDIANA

Alexandria Eschate

PUNJAB

Alexandria (Merv)

Bactra (Balkh)

BACTRIA

Alexandria

Damghan

PARTHIA

Taxila

Alexandria (Herat)

Alexandria (Ghazni)

Bucephala

Indus

Hydaspes

Occupied 331

Alexandria (Kandahar)

Alexandria

Persepolis

PERSIAN GULF

GEDROSIA

Victory over Indian king Porus 326

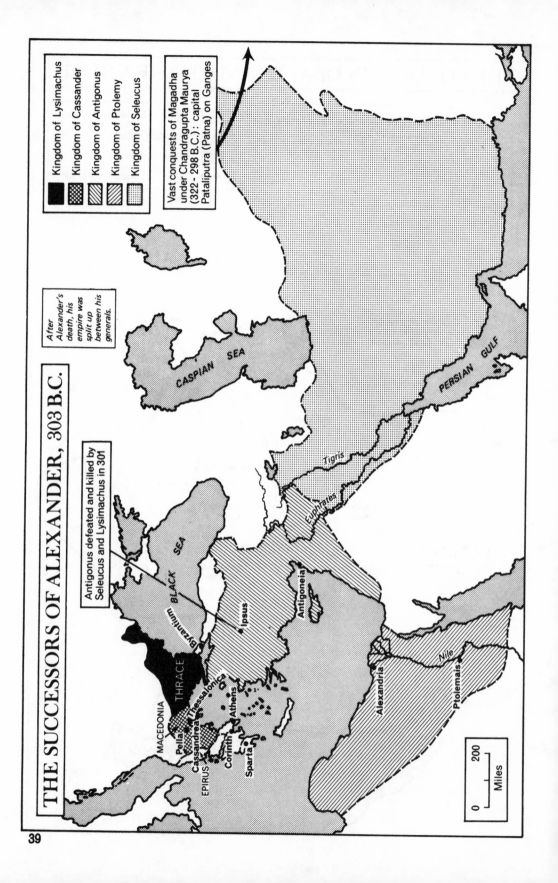

THE SUCCESSORS OF ALEXANDER, 303 B.C.

Kingdom of Lysimachus
Kingdom of Cassander
Kingdom of Antigonus
Kingdom of Ptolemy
Kingdom of Seleucus

Vast conquests of Magadha under Chandragupta Maurya (322 - 298 B.C.): capital Pataliputra (Patna) on Ganges

After Alexander's death, his empire was split up between his generals.

Antigonus defeated and killed by Seleucus and Lysimachus in 301

CASPIAN SEA

PERSIAN GULF

Tigris

Euphrates

BLACK SEA

Byzantium

Ipsus

Antigoneia

THRACE

MACEDONIA

Pella
Cassandrea
Thessalonica
EPIRUS
Corinth Athens
Sparta

Alexandria

Nile

Ptolemais

0   200
Miles

39

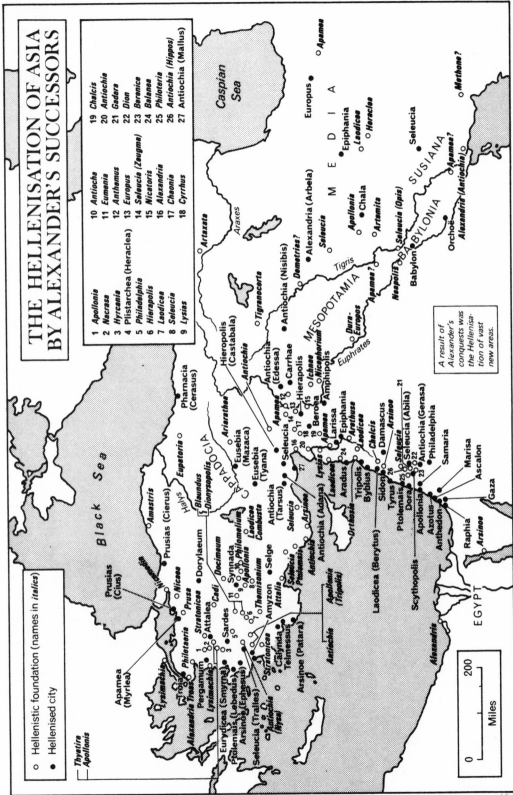

THE HELLENISATION OF ASIA
BY ALEXANDER'S SUCCESSORS

1	*Apollonia*	10	*Antiocha*
2	*Nacrasa*	11	*Eumenia*
3	*Hyrcania*	12	*Anthemus*
4	*Plistarchea (Heraclea)*	13	*Europus*
5	*Philadelphia*	14	*Seleucia (Zeugma)*
6	*Hierapolis*	15	*Nicatoris*
7	*Laodicea*	16	*Alexandria*
8	*Seleucia*	17	*Chaonia*
9	*Lysias*	18	*Cyrrhus*
		19	*Chalcis*
		20	*Antiochia*
		21	*Gadara*
		22	*Dion*
		23	*Berenice*
		24	*Balanea*
		25	*Philoteria*
		26	*Antiochia (Hippos)*
		27	*Antiochia (Mallus)*

○ Hellenistic foundation (names in *italics*)

● Hellenised city

Thyatira
Apollonis

A result of Alexander's conquests was the Hellenisation of vast new areas.

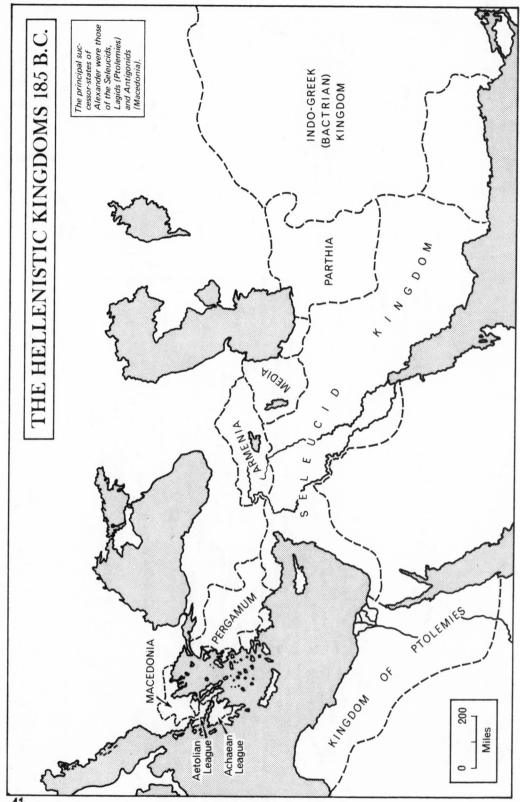

THE HELLENISTIC KINGDOMS 185 B.C.

The principal successor-states of Alexander were those of the Seleucids, Lagids (Ptolemies) and Antigonids (Macedonia).

INDO-GREEK (BACTRIAN) KINGDOM

PARTHIA

MEDIA

ARMENIA

SELEUCID KINGDOM

MACEDONIA

PERGAMUM

Aetolian League

Achaean League

KINGDOM OF PTOLEMIES

0   200
Miles

41

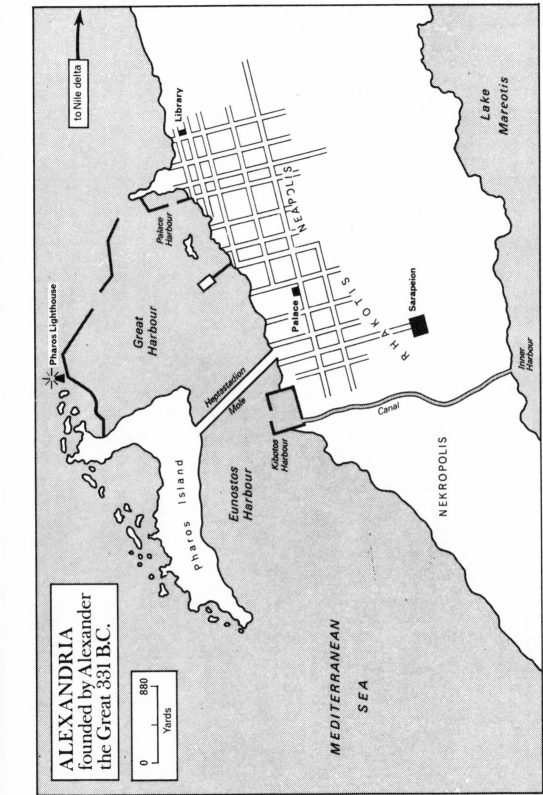

ALEXANDRIA
founded by Alexander
the Great 331 B.C.

0   880
Yards

to Nile delta

Library

NEAPOLIS

Palace

Palace
Harbour

Great
Harbour

Pharos Lighthouse

Heptastadion

Mole

Eunostos
Harbour

Kibotos
Harbour

P h a r o s   I s l a n d

R H A K O T I S

Sarapeion

Canal

Inner
Harbour

Lake
Mareotis

NEKROPOLIS

MEDITERRANEAN
SEA

42

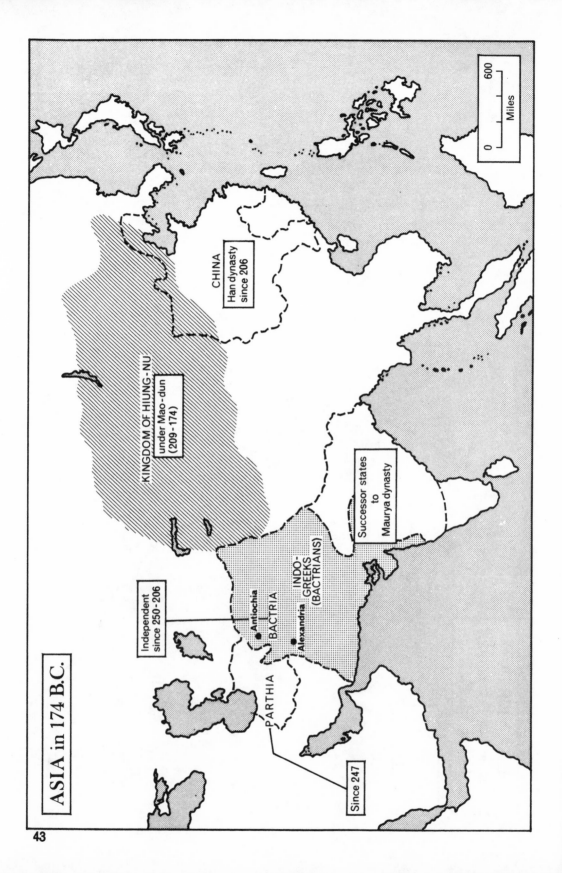

ASIA in 174 B.C.

KINGDOM OF HIUNG-NU
under Mao-dun
(209-174)

CHINA
Han dynasty
since 206

Successor states
to
Maurya dynasty

Independent
since 250-206

Antiochia

BACTRIA

Alexandria

INDO-
GREEKS
(BACTRIANS)

PARTHIA

Since 247

600

Miles

0

43

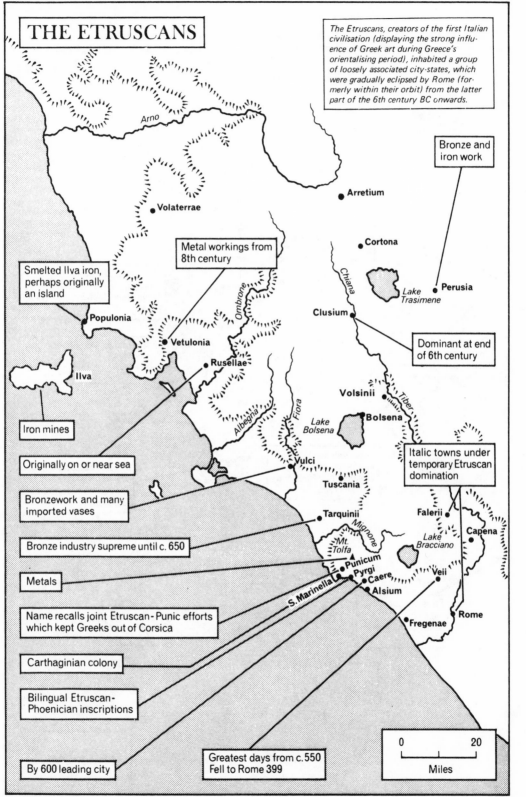

THE ETRUSCANS

The Etruscans, creators of the first Italian civilisation (displaying the strong influence of Greek art during Greece's orientalising period), inhabited a group of loosely associated city-states, which were gradually eclipsed by Rome (formerly within their orbit) from the latter part of the 6th century BC onwards.

Arno

Bronze and iron work

● **Arretium**

● **Volaterrae**

● **Cortona**

Metal workings from 8th century

Ombrone

Chiana

● **Perusia**

Lake Trasimene

Smelted Ilva iron, perhaps originally an island

● **Populonia**

● **Clusium**

Dominant at end of 6th century

● **Vetulonia**

● **Rusellae**

Ilva

Albegna

Fiora

Volsinii

Tiber

● **Bolsena**

Lake Bolsena

Iron mines

Originally on or near sea

● **Vulci**

Italic towns under temporary Etruscan domination

Bronzework and many imported vases

Tuscania

● **Falerii**

Bronze industry supreme until c. 650

● **Tarquinii**

Mignone

Lake Bracciano

● **Capena**

Metals

Mt. Tolfa

● **Punicum**

● **Pyrgi**

● **Veii**

Name recalls joint Etruscan-Punic efforts which kept Greeks out of Corsica

S. Marinella

● **Caere**

● **Alsium**

Carthaginian colony

● **Rome**

● **Fregenae**

Bilingual Etruscan-Phoenician inscriptions

By 600 leading city

Greatest days from c. 550
Fell to Rome 399

0   20

Miles

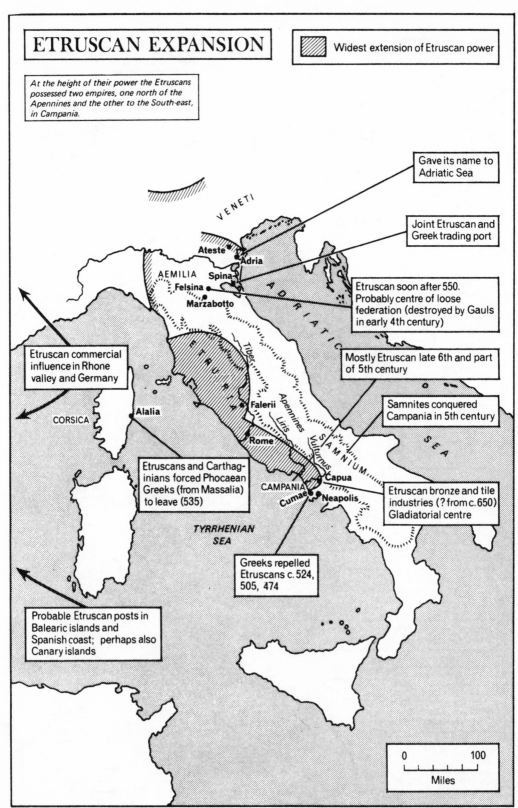

ETRUSCAN EXPANSION

Widest extension of Etruscan power

At the height of their power the Etruscans possessed two empires, one north of the Apennines and the other to the South-east, in Campania.

Gave its name to Adriatic Sea

Joint Etruscan and Greek trading port

Etruscan soon after 550. Probably centre of loose federation (destroyed by Gauls in early 4th century)

Mostly Etruscan late 6th and part of 5th century

Etruscan commercial influence in Rhone valley and Germany

Samnites conquered Campania in 5th century

Etruscans and Carthaginians forced Phocaean Greeks (from Massalia) to leave (535)

Etruscan bronze and tile industries (? from c. 650) Gladiatorial centre

Greeks repelled Etruscans c. 524, 505, 474

Probable Etruscan posts in Balearic islands and Spanish coast; perhaps also Canary islands

VENETI
Ateste
Adria
AEMILIA   Spina
Felsina
Marzabotto
ADRIATIC
E T R U R I A
Tiber
Falerii
Apennines
Liris
Rome
S A M N I U M
Volturnus
CORSICA
Alalia
SEA
Capua
CAMPANIA
Cumae   Neapolis
TYRRHENIAN SEA

0   100
Miles

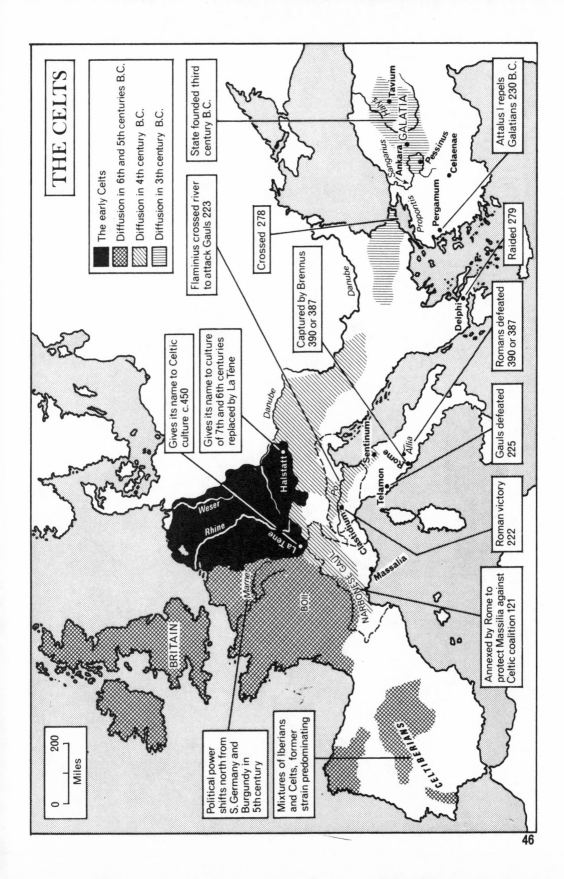

THE CELMS

The early Celts

Diffusion in 6th and 5th centuries B.C.

Diffusion in 4th century B.C.

Diffusion in 3rd century B.C.

State founded third century B.C.

Attalus I repels Galatians 230 B.C.

Flaminius crossed river to attack Gauls 223

Crossed 278

Raided 279

Captured by Brennus 390 or 387

Romans defeated 390 or 387

Gives its name to Celtic culture c.450

Gives its name to culture of 7th and 6th centuries replaced by La Tène

Gauls defeated 225

Roman victory 222

Political power shifts north from S. Germany and Burgundy in 5th century

Mixtures of Iberians and Celts, former strain predominating

Annexed by Rome to protect Massilia against Celtic coalition 121

GALATIA

Tavium

Sangarius
Ankara
Halys
Pessinus
Celaenae
Pergamum

Propontis

Delphi

Danube

Danube

Halstatt

Weser

Rhine

La Tène

Sentinum

Rome
Allia

Po
Telamon

BOII

BRITAIN

Marne

CISALPINE GAUL

NARBONNESE GAUL

Massilia

CELTIBERIANS

0   200
Miles

46

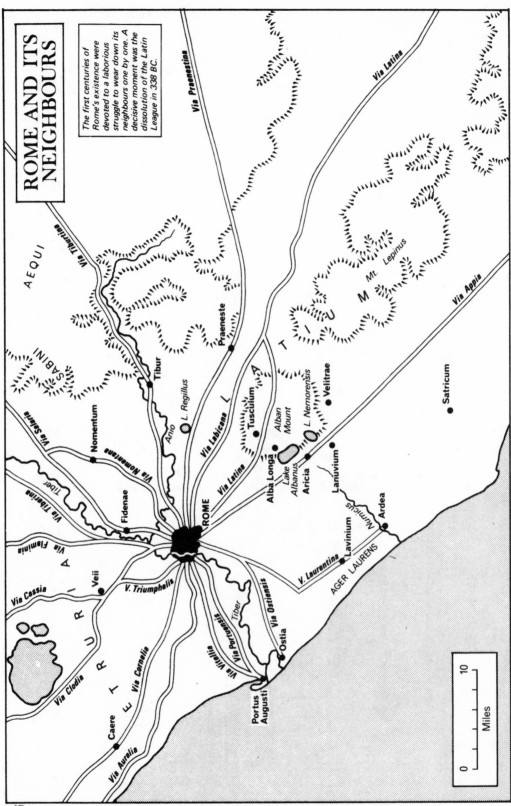

ROME AND ITS NEIGHBOURS

The first centuries of Rome's existence were devoted to a laborious struggle to wear down its neighbours one by one. A decisive moment was the dissolution of the Latin League in 338 BC.

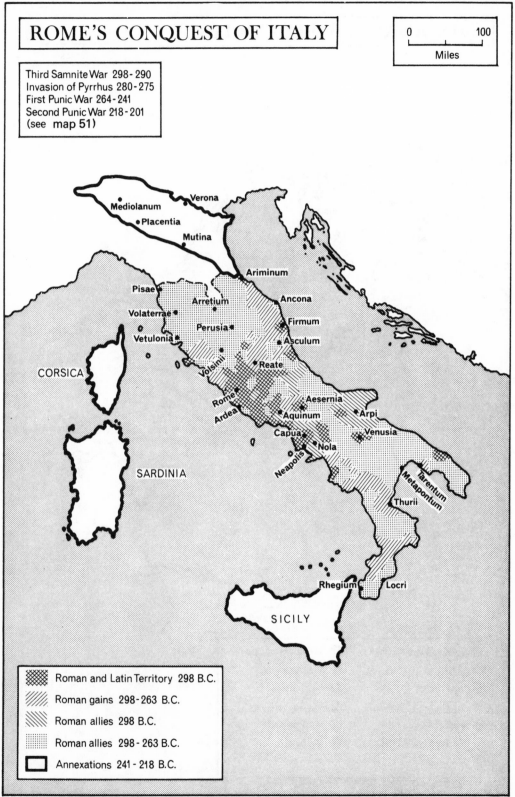

ROME'S CONQUEST OF ITALY

0   100

Miles

Third Samnite War 298-290
Invasion of Pyrrhus 280-275
First Punic War 264-241
Second Punic War 218-201
(see map 51)

Verona

Mediolanum

Placentia

Mutina

Ariminum

Pisae

Arretium

Ancona

Volaterrae

Perusia

Firmum

Vetulonia

Asculum

Volsinii

Reate

CORSICA

Rome

Aesernia

Ardea

Aquinum

Arpi

Capua

Venusia

Nola

SARDINIA

Neapolis

Tarentum

Metapontum

Thurii

Rhegium

Locri

SICILY

Roman and Latin Territory 298 B.C.

Roman gains 298-263 B.C.

Roman allies 298 B.C.

Roman allies 298-263 B.C.

Annexations 241-218 B.C.

THE ROADS OF ROMAN ITALY

0   100

Miles

CORSICA

SARDINIA

TYRRHENIAN SEA

ADRIATIC SEA

SICILY

Augusta Praetoria

Segusio

Mediolanum

Placentia

Cremona

Verona

Aquileia

Dertona

Genua

Mantua

Ravenna

Luna

Florentia

Ariminum

Fanum Fortunae

Pisae

Vada Volaterrana

Arretium

Truentum

Reate

Aternum

Corfinium

Tibur

ROME

Anagnia

Fregellae

Tarracina

Cales

Capua

Casilinum

Neapolis

Beneventum

Canusium

Venusia

Brundisium

Tarentum

Rhegium

Po

1	Via Aemilia (187 B.C.)	8	Via Julia Augusta
2	Via Appia (312 - 244 B.C.)	9	Via Domitiana
3	Via Aurelia	10	Via Trajana
4	Via Flaminia (220 B.C.)	11	Via Cassia
5	Via Latina	12	Via Popillia
6	Via Postumia (148 B.C.)	13	Via Salaria
7	Via Valeria		

49

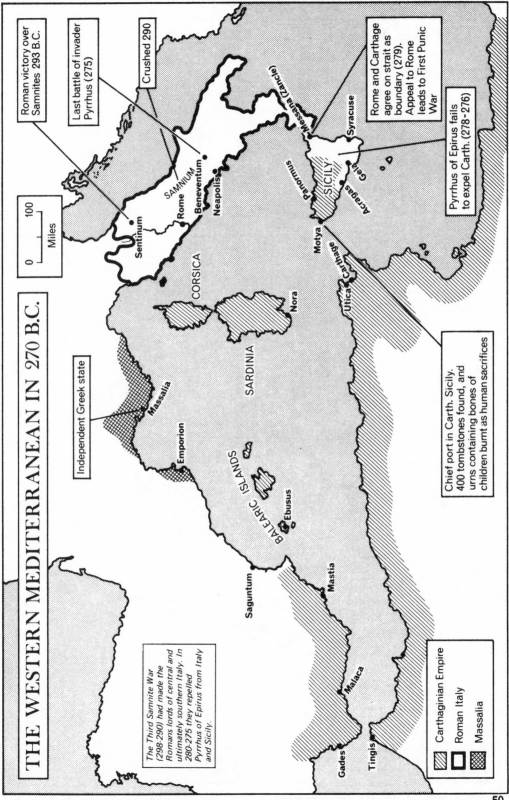

THE WESTERN MEDITERRANEAN IN 270 B.C.

Roman victory over Samnites 293 B.C.

Last battle of invader Pyrrhus (275)

Crushed 290

Rome and Carthage agree on strait as boundary (279). Appeal to Rome leads to First Punic War

Pyrrhus of Epirus fails to expel Carth. (278-276)

Independent Greek state

Chief port in Carth. Sicily. 400 tombstones found, and urns containing bones of children burnt as human sacrifices

The Third Samnite War (298-290) had made the Romans lords of central and ultimately southern Italy. In 280-275 they repelled Pyrrhus of Epirus from Italy and Sicily.

0 100
Miles

SAMNIUM
Rome
Sentinum
Beneventum
Neapolis
Messana (Zancle)
Panormus
SICILY
Syracuse
Gela
Acragas
Motya
Utica
Carthage

CORSICA
Nora
SARDINIA

Massalia
Emporion
BALEARIC ISLANDS
Ebusus

Saguntum
Mastia

Malaca
Gades
Tingis

Carthaginian Empire

Roman Italy

Massalia

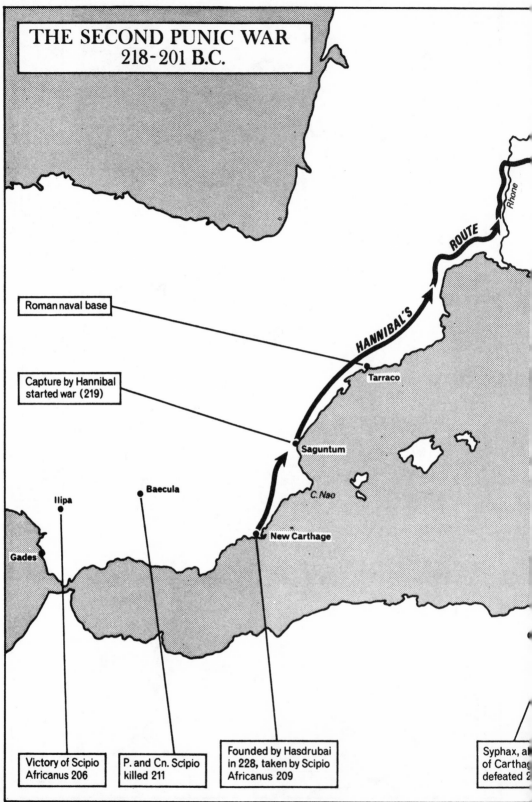

THE SECOND PUNIC WAR
218-201 B.C.

Roman naval base

Capture by Hannibal started war (219)

HANNIBAL'S ROUTE

Rhone

Tarraco

Saguntum

C. Nao

Ilipa

Baecula

Gades

New Carthage

Victory of Scipio Africanus 206

P. and Cn. Scipio killed 211

Founded by Hasdrubai in 228, taken by Scipio Africanus 209

Syphax, a of Carthag defeated 2

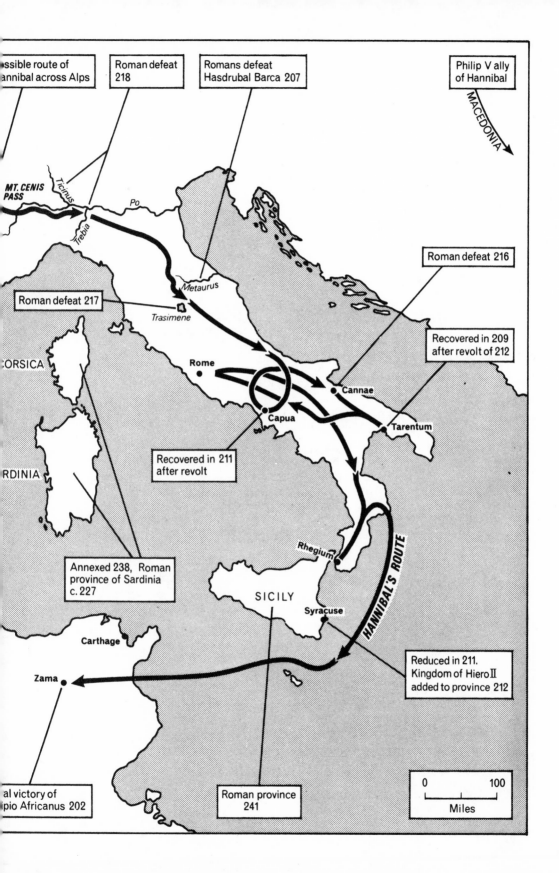

ssible route of
annibal across Alps

Roman defeat
218

Romans defeat
Hasdrubal Barca 207

Philip V ally
of Hannibal

MACEDONIA

MT. CENIS
PASS

Ticinus

Po

Trebia

Metaurus

Roman defeat 217

Trasimene

Roman defeat 216

CORSICA

Rome

Recovered in 209
after revolt of 212

Cannae

RDINIA

Capua

Tarentum

Recovered in 211
after revolt

Annexed 238, Roman
province of Sardinia
c. 227

Rhegium

HANNIBAL'S ROUTE

SICILY

Syracuse

Reduced in 211.
Kingdom of Hiero II
added to province 212

Carthage

Zama

al victory of
ipio Africanus 202

Roman province
241

0   100

Miles

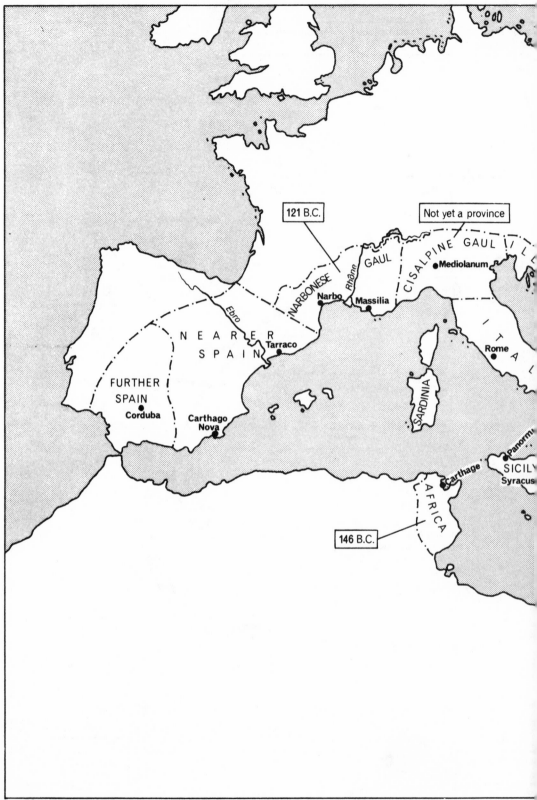

121 B.C.

Not yet a province

GAUL

NARBONESE

CISALPINE GAUL

Mediolanum

Rhône

Ebro

Narbo

Massilia

N E A R E R
S P A I N

Tarraco

Rome

FURTHER
SPAIN

Corduba

Carthago
Nova

SARDINIA

Panorm

SICILY

Carthage

Syracuse

AFRICA

146 B.C.

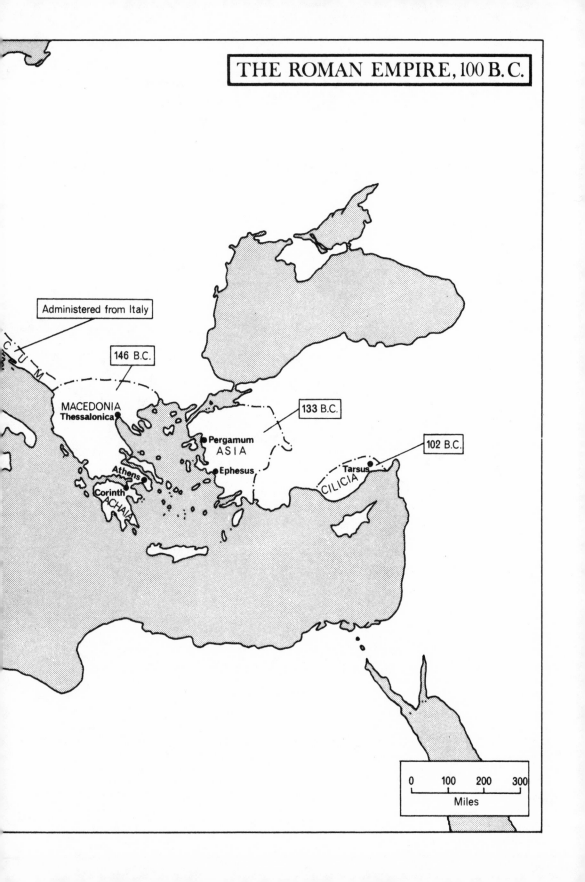

THE ROMAN EMPIRE, 100 B.C.

Administered from Italy

146 B.C.

133 B.C.

102 B.C.

MACEDONIA
Thessalonica

Pergamum
ASIA

Ephesus

Tarsus
CILICIA

Athens

Corinth
ACHAIA

| 0 | 100 | 200 | 300 |
Miles

BRITANNIA

GAUL
(GALLIA COMATA)

Citizenship granted 49,
province 42 B.C.

Conquered by
Caesar 58-51 B.C.

Lugdunum

CISALPINE GAUL

Mediolanum

ILLY

Rhine

NARBONESE GAUL

Rubicon

Narbo

Massilia

Rhone

Ebro

Ilerda

Tarraco

FURTHER
SPAIN

NEARER
SPAIN

Rome

ITALY

Cordoba

Munda

SARDINIA

Panormus

Carthage

Syracuse

SICILY

Cirta

AFRICA NOVA

AFRICA

Thapsus

Province 46-30 B.C.

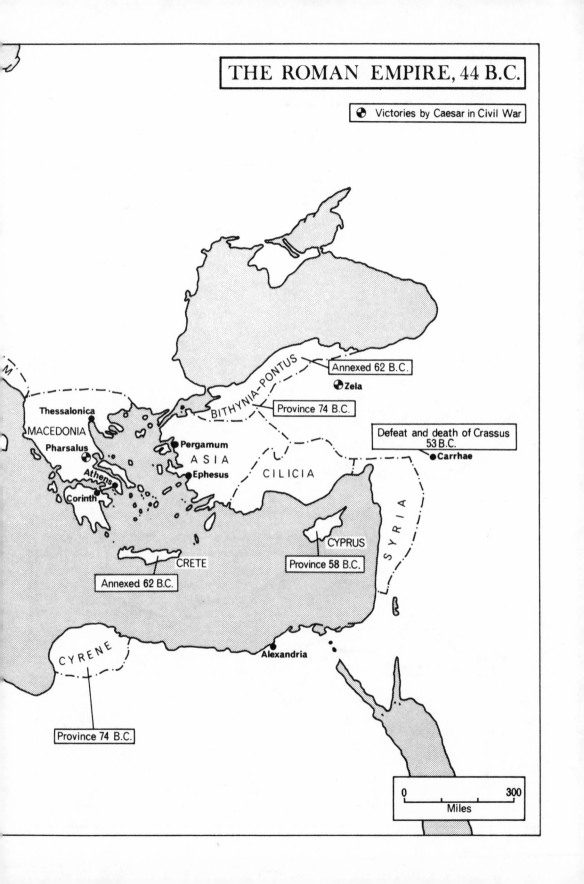

THE ROMAN EMPIRE, 44 B.C.

🌐 Victories by Caesar in Civil War

Annexed 62 B.C.

🌐 **Zela**

BITHYNIA-PONTUS

Province 74 B.C.

Thessalonica

MACEDONIA

Pharsalus

A S I A

Pergamum

Athens

Ephesus

CILICIA

Defeat and death of Crassus
53 B.C.

Carrhae

S Y R I A

Corinth

CYPRUS

CRETE

Province 58 B.C.

Annexed 62 B.C.

C Y R E N E

Alexandria

Province 74 B.C.

0   300

Miles

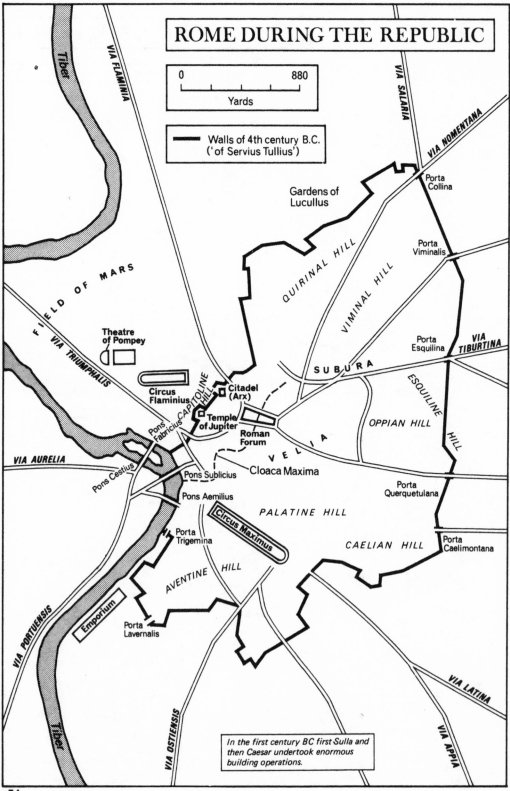

ROME DURING THE REPUBLIC

0   880

Yards

Walls of 4th century B.C.
('of Servius Tullius')

Tiber

VIA FLAMINIA

VIA SALARIA

VIA NOMENTANA

Porta
Collina

Gardens of
Lucullus

Porta
Viminalis

QUIRINAL HILL

VIMINAL HILL

F I E L D   O F   M A R S

Porta
Esquilina

VIA
TIBURTINA

VIA TRIUMPHALIS

Theatre
of Pompey

SUBURA

ESQUILINE HILL

Circus
Flaminius

CAPITOLINE HILL

Citadel
(Arx)

OPPIAN HILL

Pons Fabricius

Temple
of Jupiter

Roman
Forum

V E L I A

VIA AURELIA

Pons Cestius

Pons Sublicius

Cloaca Maxima

Porta
Querquetulana

Pons Aemilius

PALATINE HILL

Circus Maximus

Porta
Trigemina

CAELIAN HILL

Porta
Caelimontana

VIA PORTUENSIS

Emporium

AVENTINE   HILL

Porta
Lavernalis

VIA OSTIENSIS

VIA LATINA

VIA APPIA

Tiber

In the first century BC first Sulla and
then Caesar undertook enormous
building operations.

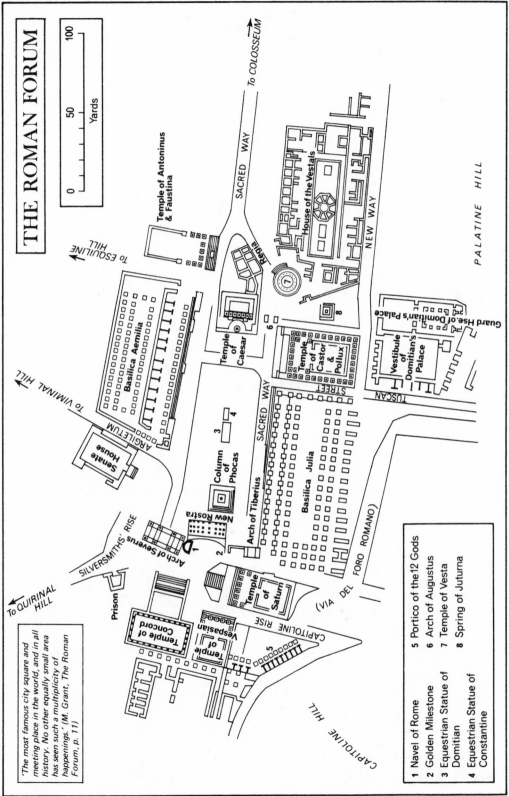

THE ROMAN FORUM

Yards

0 · · · · 50 · · · · 100

'The most famous city square and
meeting place in the world, and in all
history. No other equally small area
has seen such a multiplicity of
happenings.' (M. Grant, The Roman
Forum, p. 11)

To ESQUILINE HILL

Temple of Antoninus
& Faustina

SACRED WAY

To COLOSSEUM

Regia

House of the Vestals

NEW WAY

PALATINE HILL

To VIMINAL HILL

Basilica Aemilia

ARGILETUM

Senate
House

Temple
of Caesar

Temple
of
Castor
&
Pollux

Guard Hse. of Domitian's Palace

Vestibule
of
Domitian's
Palace

TUSCAN STREET

SILVERSMITHS' RISE

Column
of
Phocas

3

4

New Rostra

SACRED WAY

Basilica Julia

To QUIRINAL HILL

Arch of Severus

Arch of Tiberius

1

2

(VIA DEL FORO ROMANO)

Prison

Temple of
Concord

Temple
of
Vespasian

Temple
of
Saturn

5

CAPITOLINE RISE

CAPITOLINE HILL

1 Navel of Rome
2 Golden Milestone
3 Equestrian Statue of
   Domitian
4 Equestrian Statue of
   Constantine

5 Portico of the 12 Gods
6 Arch of Augustus
7 Temple of Vesta
8 Spring of Juturna

55

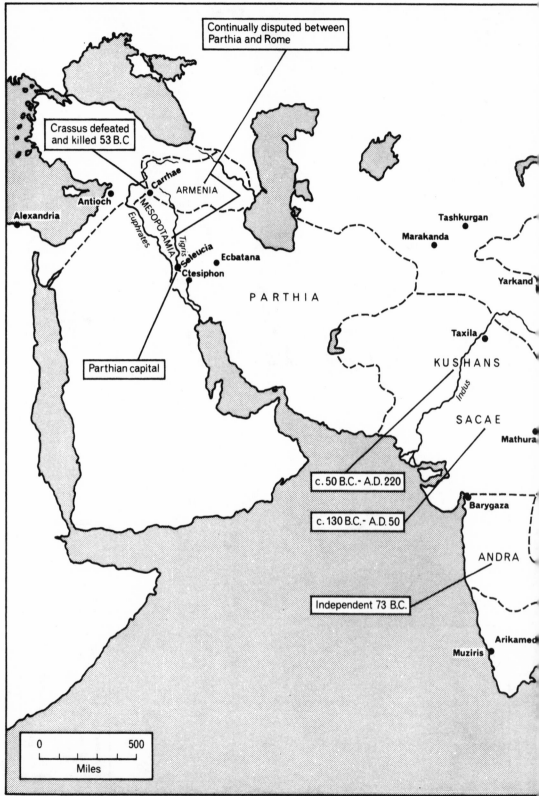

Continually disputed between
Parthia and Rome

Crassus defeated
and killed 53 B.C

ARMENIA

Carrhae

Antioch

Alexandria

MESOPOTAMIA

Euphrates

Tigris

Seleucia

Ecbatana

Ctesiphon

Parthian capital

PARTHIA

Tashkurgan

Marakanda

Yarkand

Taxila

KUSHANS

Indus

SACAE

Mathura

c. 50 B.C.- A.D. 220

c. 130 B.C.- A.D. 50

Barygaza

ANDRA

Independent 73 B.C.

Arikamed

Muziris

0   500

Miles

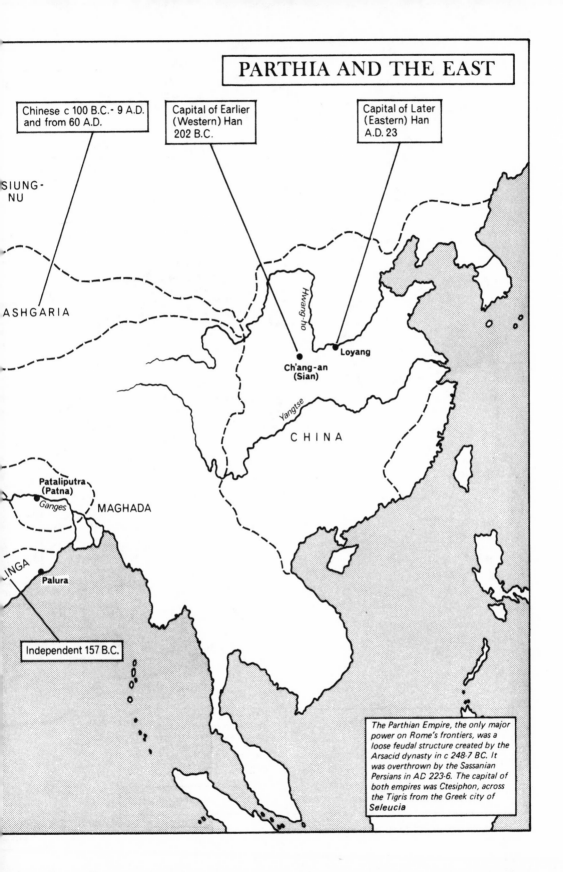

PARTHIA AND THE EAST

Chinese c 100 B.C.- 9 A.D. and from 60 A.D.

Capital of Earlier (Western) Han 202 B.C.

Capital of Later (Eastern) Han A.D. 23

SIUNG-NU

ASHGARIA

Hwang-ho

Loyang

Ch'ang-an (Sian)

Yangtse

CHINA

Pataliputra (Patna)

Ganges

MAGHADA

LINGA

Palura

Independent 157 B.C.

The Parthian Empire, the only major power on Rome's frontiers, was a loose feudal structure created by the Arsacid dynasty in c 248-7 BC. It was overthrown by the Sassanian Persians in AD 223-6. The capital of both empires was Ctesiphon, across the Tigris from the Greek city of *Seleucia*

BRITANNIA

FREE
GERMANY

LWR.
GERMANY
(17 B.C.)

Temporarily conquered from
15 B.C. but abandoned after
ambushing of Varus by
Arminius in A.D. 9

Colonia
Agrippinensis

Rhine

B E L G I C A

Moguntiacum

Danube

LOWER
PANNONIA
(10
B.C

LUGDUNENSIS

RHAETIA
(15 B.C.)

NORICUM
(15 B.C.)

UPPER
PANNONIA

UPR.
GERMANY
(17 B.C.)

Lugdunum

P

Aquileia

AQUITANIA

C

I
T
A
L
Y

Adriatic
Sea

NARBONENSIS

M

Nemausus

Rome

TARRACONENSIS

Tarraco

LUSITANIA
(c. 27 B.C.)

Corduba

BAETICA

Naulochus

SICILY

Gades

Carthage

M A U R E T A N I A

Naval victory over
Sextus Pompeius
36 B.C.

A
F
R
I
C
A

Imperial frontier as in A.D. 14

Provincial frontiers

ASIA   Senatorial provinces

ALPINE PROVINCES (15-14 B.C.)
M: Maritime, C: Cottian, P: Pennine

The hatched areas represent the
more important dependent ('client')
states, whose monarchs enjoyed
internal autonomy but had to
support Rome's foreign policy and
help defend the imperial frontiers.

///// Principal client states

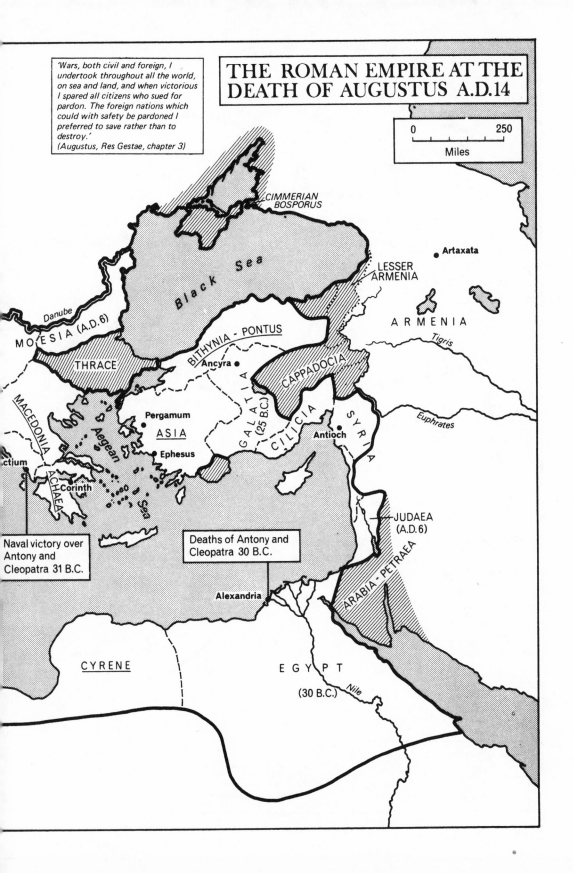

THE ROMAN EMPIRE AT THE
DEATH OF AUGUSTUS A.D.14

'Wars, both civil and foreign, I
undertook throughout all the world,
on sea and land, and when victorious
I spared all citizens who sued for
pardon. The foreign nations which
could with safety be pardoned I
preferred to save rather than to
destroy.'
(Augustus, Res Gestae, chapter 3)

0   250
Miles

CIMMERIAN
BOSPORUS

• Artaxata

Black Sea

LESSER
ARMENIA

ARMENIA

Danube

MOESIA (A.D.6)

Tigris

THRACE

BITHYNIA - PONTUS

Ancyra •

CAPPADOCIA

MACEDONIA

Pergamum

ASIA

GALATIA
(25 B.C.)

CILICIA

SYRIA

Euphrates

Antioch

Aegean Sea

Ephesus

Actium

ACHAEA

Corinth

JUDAEA
(A.D.6)

Naval victory over
Antony and
Cleopatra 31 B.C.

Deaths of Antony and
Cleopatra 30 B.C.

ARABIA - PETRAEA

Alexandria

CYRENE

EGYPT

(30 B.C.)

Nile

All roads lead to Rome: the most potent guarantees of external and internal peace and stimulants of prosperity.

Imperial frontier as in A.D. 14
Roman roads
Mountain contours

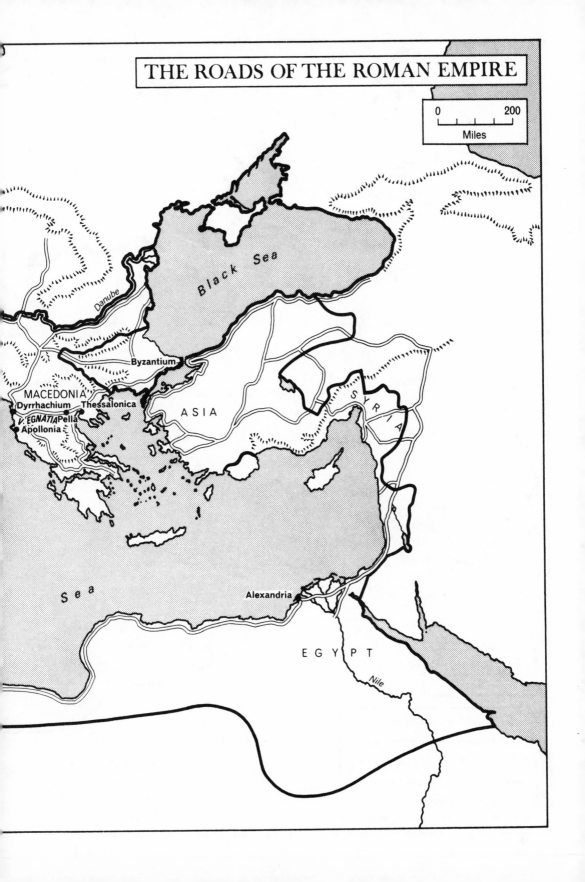

THE ROADS OF THE ROMAN EMPIRE

0   200
Miles

Black Sea

Danube

Byzantium

MACEDONIA
Dyrrhachium   Thessalonica
V. EGNATIA Pella
Apollonia

ASIA

SYRIA

Sea

Alexandria

EGYPT

Nile

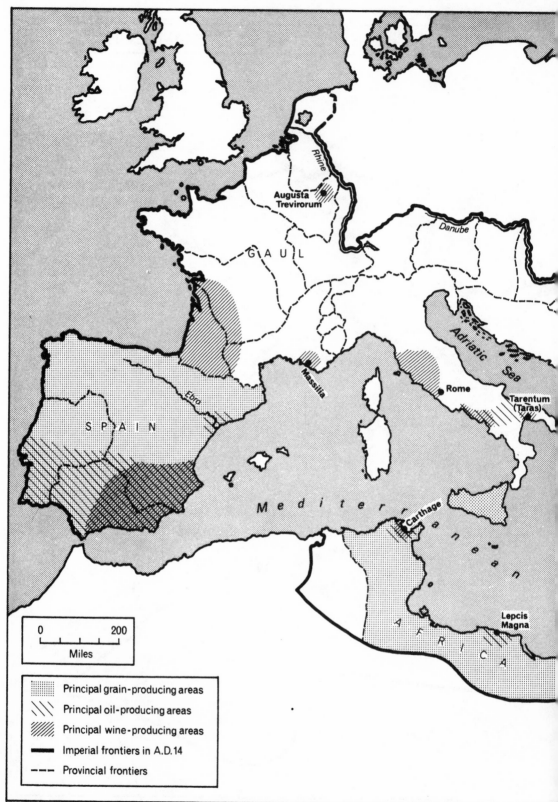

Rhine

Augusta
Trevirorum

Danube

G A U L

Adriatic Sea

Massilia

Rome

Tarentum
(Taras)

Ebro

S P A I N

Mediterranean

Carthage

Lepcis
Magna

A F R I C A

0   200
Miles

Principal grain-producing areas

Principal oil-producing areas

Principal wine-producing areas

Imperial frontiers in A.D.14

Provincial frontiers

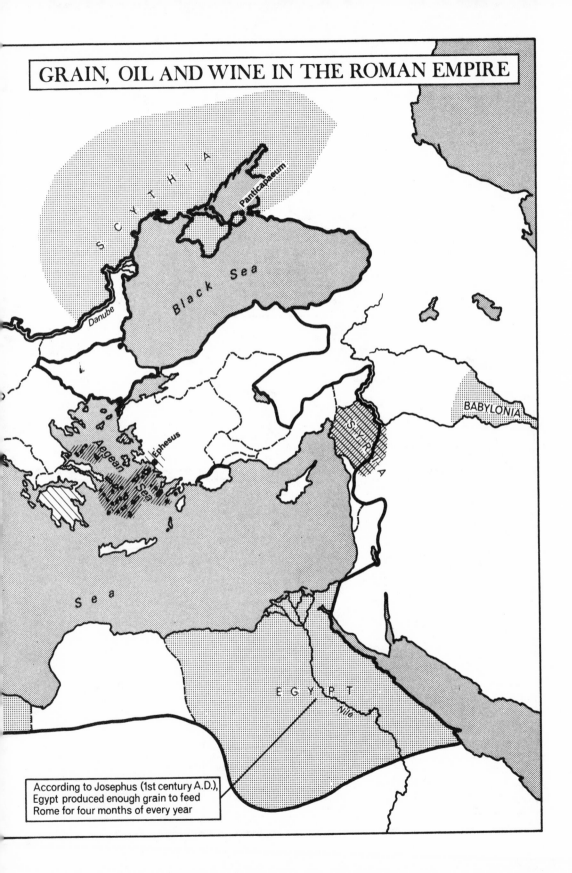

GRAIN, OIL AND WINE IN THE ROMAN EMPIRE

S C Y T H I A

Panticapaeum

Danube

Black Sea

BABYLONIA

S Y R I A

Aegean Sea

Ephesus

Sea

E G Y P T

Nile

According to Josephus (1st century A.D.),
Egypt produced enough grain to feed
Rome for four months of every year

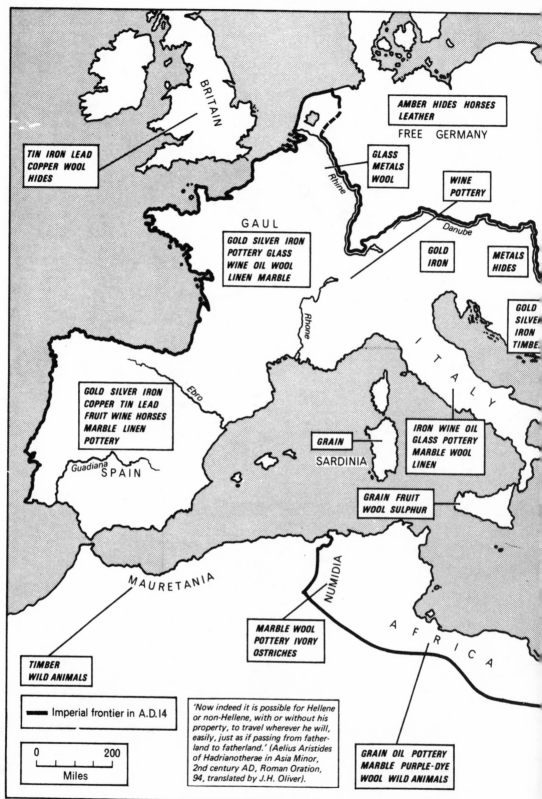

BRITAIN

TIN IRON LEAD COPPER WOOL HIDES

AMBER HIDES HORSES LEATHER

FREE GERMANY

GLASS METALS WOOL

Rhine

WINE POTTERY

GAUL

GOLD SILVER IRON POTTERY GLASS WINE OIL WOOL LINEN MARBLE

Danube

GOLD IRON

METALS HIDES

Rhone

I T A L Y

GOLD SILVER IRON TIMBE.

Ebro

GOLD SILVER IRON COPPER TIN LEAD FRUIT WINE HORSES MARBLE LINEN POTTERY

GRAIN

SARDINIA

IRON WINE OIL GLASS POTTERY MARBLE WOOL LINEN

Guadiana SPAIN

GRAIN FRUIT WOOL SULPHUR

MAURETANIA

NUMIDIA

A F R I C A

MARBLE WOOL POTTERY IVORY OSTRICHES

TIMBER WILD ANIMALS

━━━ Imperial frontier in A.D.14

0   200
Miles

'Now indeed it is possible for Hellene or non-Hellene, with or without his property, to travel wherever he will, easily, just as if passing from father-land to fatherland.' (Aelius Aristides of Hadrianotherae in Asia Minor, 2nd century AD, Roman Oration, 94, translated by J.H. Oliver).

GRAIN OIL POTTERY MARBLE PURPLE-DYE WOOL WILD ANIMALS

TRADING PRODUCTS IN THE ROMAN EMPIRE

GRAIN HONEY HEMP NUTS HIDES

GOLD TIMBER HORSES SALT

IRON

CAUCASUS

SILK from China

ARMENIA — IRON

GRAIN FISH GOLD SILVER IRON LEAD

METALS BITUMEN PRECIOUS STONES

DACIA

SCYTHIA

Dnieper

Dniester

Bug

Danube

Black Sea

MESOPOTAMIA

Tigris

MOESIA

THRACE

GRAIN FISH HORSES

ASIA

WOOL LINEN WINE OIL MARBLE POTTERY PARCHMENT TIMBER HORSES EMERALDS GOLD SILVER IRON

SYRIA

Euphrates

SILK from China

MACEDONIA

GREECE

CYPRUS

COPPER OIL

JUDAEA

WOOL PURPLE-DYE LINEN GLASS POTTERY TIMBER LEATHER-GOODS

WINE HONEY LINEN PURPLE-DYE POTTERY MARBLE

ARABIA

ASPHALT

FRANKINCENSE AND OTHER PERFUMES

to South Arabia

EGYPT

PEPPER from India

CYRENE

GLASS GRAIN LINEN TEXTILES DRUGS PAPYRUS WILD ANIMALS PORPHYRY

IVORY from Central Africa

SILPHIUM [Medicinal herb] TIMBER

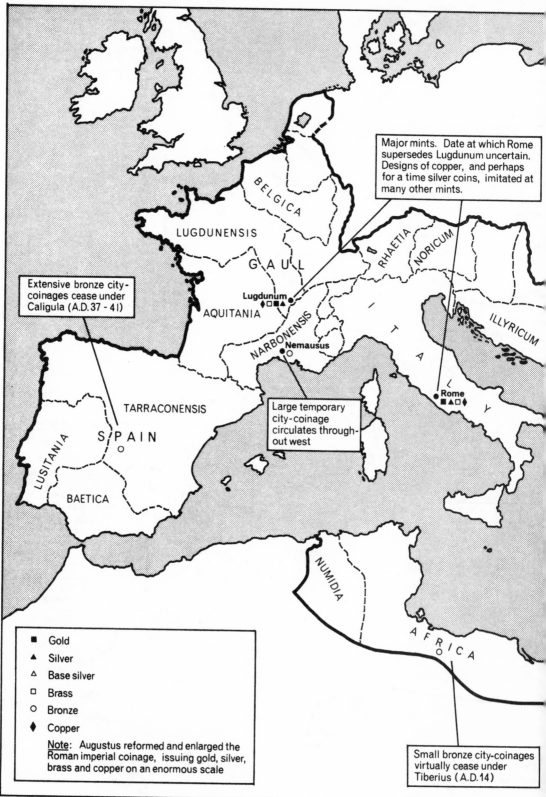

Major mints. Date at which Rome supersedes Lugdunum uncertain. Designs of copper, and perhaps for a time silver coins, imitated at many other mints.

Extensive bronze city-coinages cease under Caligula (A.D. 37 - 41)

Large temporary city-coinage circulates throughout west

BELGICA

LUGDUNENSIS

GAUL

AQUITANIA

Lugdunum
◆ □ ■ ▲

NARBONENSIS

Nemausus
○

RHAETIA   NORICUM

I
T
A
L
Y

ILLYRICUM

Rome
● ■ ▲ □ ◆

TARRACONENSIS

S P A I N
○

LUSITANIA

BAETICA

NUMIDIA

A F R I C A
○

■	Gold
▲	Silver
△	Base silver
□	Brass
○	Bronze
◆	Copper

<u>Note</u>: Augustus reformed and enlarged the Roman imperial coinage, issuing gold, silver, brass and copper on an enormous scale

Small bronze city-coinages virtually cease under Tiberius (A.D. 14)

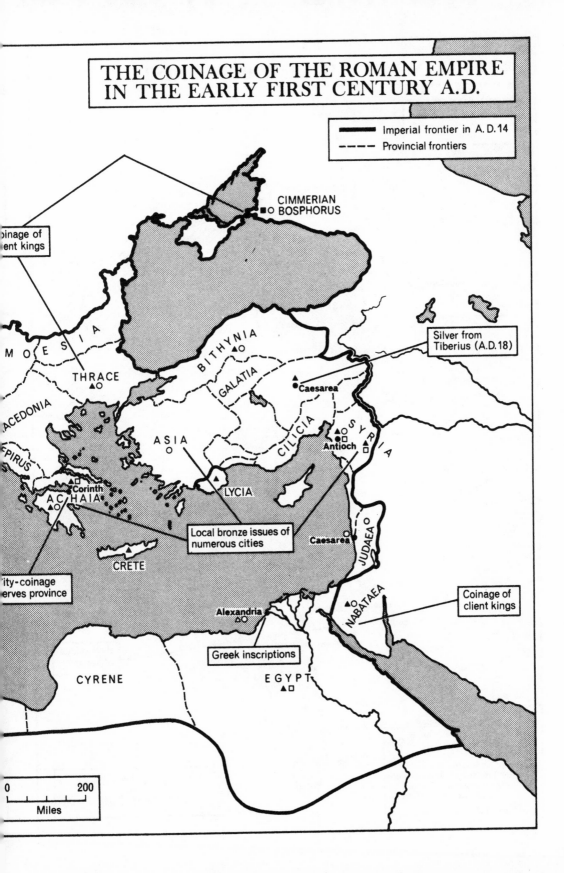

THE COINAGE OF THE ROMAN EMPIRE
IN THE EARLY FIRST CENTURY A.D.

——	Imperial frontier in A.D.14
-- -- --	Provincial frontiers

CIMMERIAN
■ ○ BOSPHORUS

oinage of
ient kings

Silver from
Tiberius (A.D.18)

M O E S I A

BITHYNIA
▲ ○

THRACE
▲ ○

GALATIA

▲
● Caesarea

ACEDONIA

ASIA
○

CILICIA

S Y R I A
▲ ○
● □ Antioch
□

EPIRUS

▲
●Corinth

LYCIA

A C H A I A
▲ ○

Local bronze issues of
numerous cities

Caesarea ○

JUDAEA ○

CRETE ▲

ity-coinage
erves province

▲ ○
NABATAEA

Coinage of
client kings

Alexandria
△ ○

Greek inscriptions

CYRENE

E G Y P T
▲ □

0	200

Miles

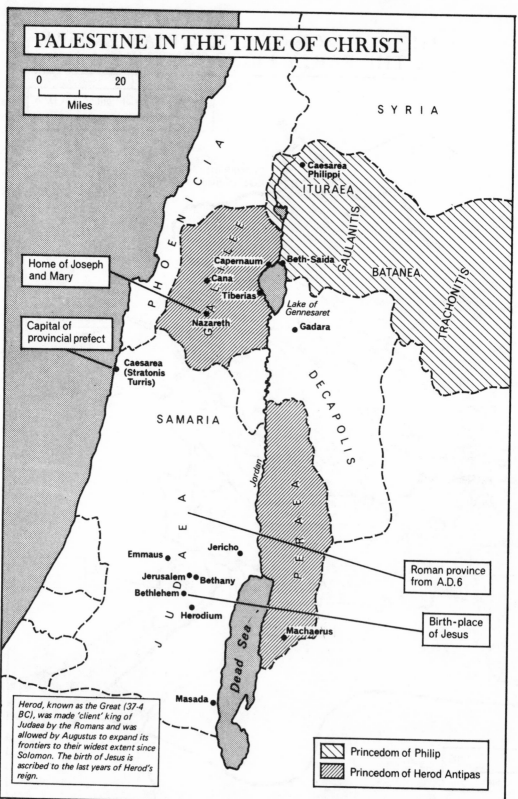

PALESTINE IN THE TIME OF CHRIST

0   20

Miles

SYRIA

PHOENICIA

ITURAEA

● Caesarea Philippi

GAULANITIS

BATANEA

TRACHONITIS

GALILEE

Capernaum ●

Cana ●

● Beth-Saida

Tiberias ●

Lake of Gennesaret

Nazareth ●

● Gadara

Home of Joseph and Mary

Capital of provincial prefect

Caesarea (Stratonis Turris) ●

SAMARIA

DECAPOLIS

Jordan

PERAEA

Emmaus ●

Jericho ●

JUDAEA

Jerusalem ● ● Bethany

Bethlehem ●

Herodium ●

● Machaerus

Dead Sea

Roman province from A.D.6

Birth-place of Jesus

Masada ●

Herod, known as the Great (37-4 BC), was made 'client' king of Judaea by the Romans and was allowed by Augustus to expand its frontiers to their widest extent since Solomon. The birth of Jesus is ascribed to the last years of Herod's reign.

Princedom of Philip

Princedom of Herod Antipas

62

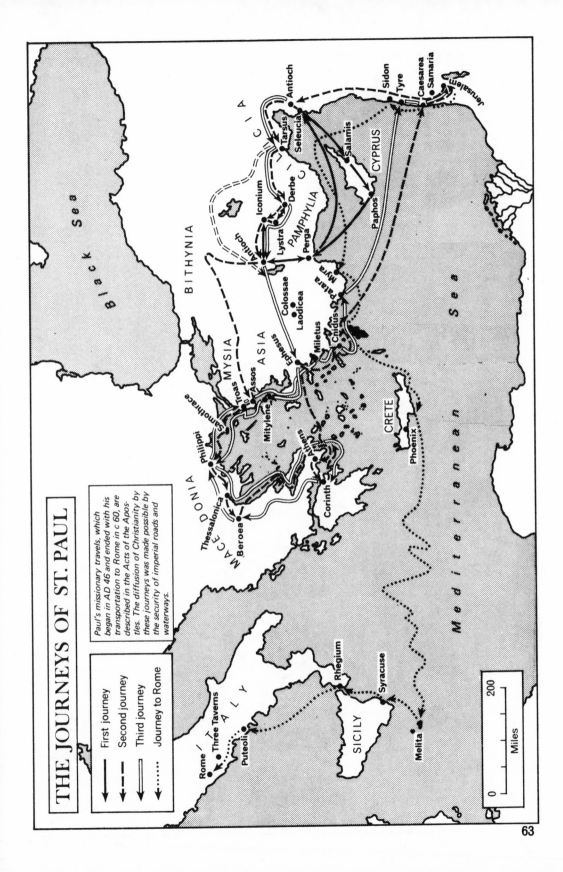

THE JOURNEYS OF ST. PAUL

Paul's missionary travels, which began in AD 46 and ended with his transportation to Rome in c 60, are described in the Acts of the Apostles. The diffusion of Christianity by these journeys was made possible by the security of imperial roads and waterways.

First journey
Second journey
Third journey
Journey to Rome

200

0

Miles

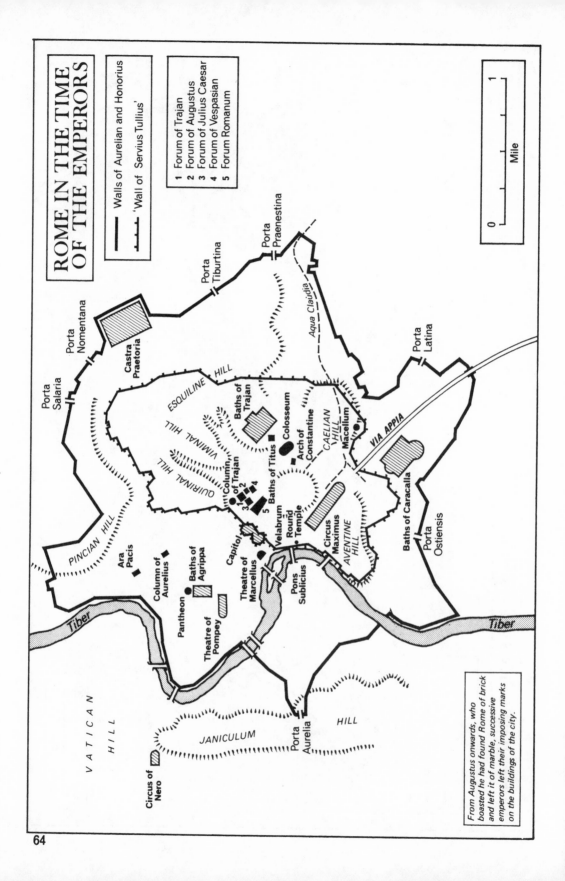

ROME IN THE TIME OF THE EMPERORS

— Walls of Aurelian and Honorius

···· 'Wall of Servius Tullius'

1 Forum of Trajan
2 Forum of Augustus
3 Forum of Julius Caesar
4 Forum of Vespasian
5 Forum Romanum

0   Mile   1

Porta Tiburtina

Porta Praenestina

Porta Nomentana

Castra Praetoria

Porta Salaria

Aqua Claudia

Porta Latina

ESQUILINE HILL

VIMINAL HILL

QUIRINAL HILL

PINCIAN HILL

Baths of Trajan

Colosseum

Arch of Constantine

CAELIAN HILL

Macellum

VIA APPIA

Baths of Titus

Column of Trajan

1
2   4
3   5

Velabrum

Round Temple

Circus Maximus

AVENTINE HILL

Baths of Caracalla

Porta Ostiensis

Ara Pacis

Column of Aurelius

Pantheon

Baths of Agrippa

Capitol

Theatre of Marcellus

Theatre of Pompey

Pons Sublicius

Tiber

Tiber

VATICAN HILL

JANICULUM

Porta Aurelia

HILL

Circus of Nero

From Augustus onwards, who boasted he had found Rome of brick and left it of marble, successive emperors left their imposing marks on the buildings of the city.

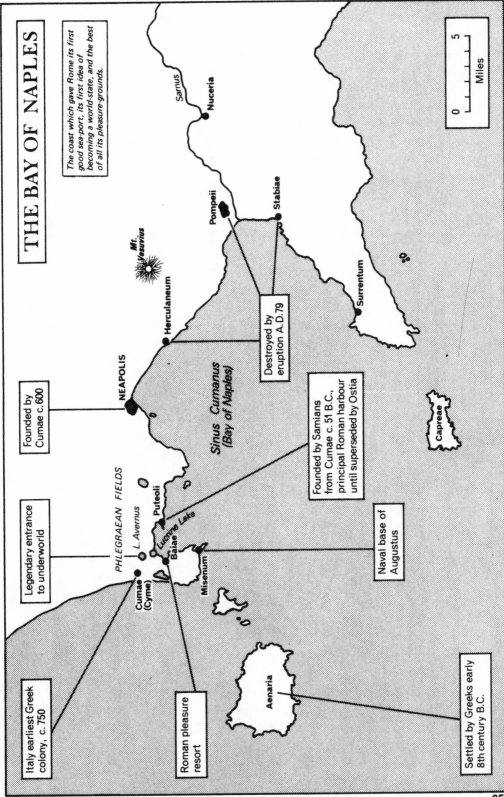

THE BAY OF NAPLES

The coast which gave Rome its first good sea-port, its first idea of becoming a world-state, and the best of all its pleasure-grounds.

Sarnus

Nuceria

Pompeii

Stabiae

Destroyed by eruption A.D. 79

Mt. Vesuvius

Herculaneum

Surrentum

NEAPOLIS

Founded by Cumae c. 600

Sinus Cumanus (Bay of Naples)

Founded by Samians from Cumae c. 51 B.C., principal Roman harbour until superseded by Ostia

Capreae

PHLEGRAEAN FIELDS

Puteoli

Legendary entrance to underworld

L. Avernus

Lucrine Lake

Baiae

Naval base of Augustus

Cumae (Cyme)

Misenum

Italy earliest Greek colony, c. 750

Roman pleasure resort

Aenaria

Settled by Greeks early 8th century B.C.

0   5
Miles

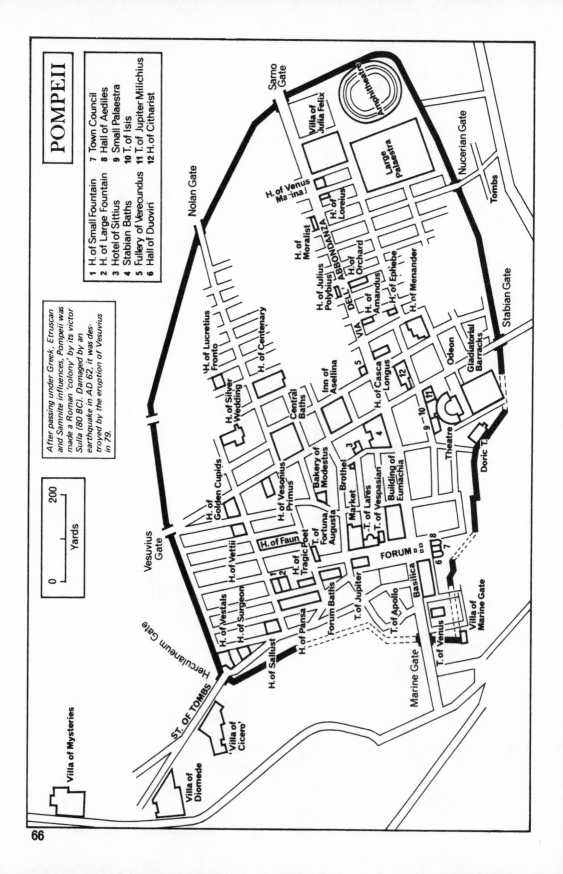

POMPEII

1 H. of Small Fountain
2 H. of Large Fountain
3 Hotel of Sittius
4 Stabian Baths
5 Fullery of Verecundus
6 Hall of Duoviri
7 Town Council
8 Hall of Aediles
9 Small Palaestra
10 T. of Isis
11 T. of Jupiter Milichius
12 H. of Citharist

After passing under Greek, Etruscan and Samnite influences, Pompeii was made a Roman 'colony' by its victor Sulla (80 BC). Damaged by an earthquake in AD 62, it was destroyed by the eruption of Vesuvius in 79.

0   200
Yards

Villa of Mysteries

Villa of Cicero

Villa of Diomede

ST. OF TOMBS

Herculaneum Gate

Vesuvius Gate

Nolan Gate

Sarno Gate

H. of Sallust
H. of Vestals
H. of Surgeon
H. of Pansa
H. of Vettii
H. of Tragic Poet
T. of Fortuna Augusta
H. of Faun
H. of Golden Cupids
H. of Vesonius Primus
Bakery of Modestus
H. of Silver Wedding
H. of Centenary
H. of Lucretius Fronto
Central Baths
Inn of Asellina
VIA DELL' ABBONDANZA
H. of Julius Polybius
H. of Moralist
H. of Venus Marina
Villa of Julia Felix
Amphitheatre
Large Palaestra
H. of Loreius
H. of Orchard
H. of Amandus
H. of Ephebe
H. of Menander
H. of Casca Longus
Odeon
Gladiatorial Barracks
Theatre
Doric T.
Building of Eumachia
T. of Vespasian
T. of Lares
Market
Brothel
Forum Baths
T. of Jupiter
FORUM
Basilica
T. of Apollo
T. of Venus
Villa of Marine Gate
Marine Gate
Stabian Gate
Nucerian Gate
Tombs

66

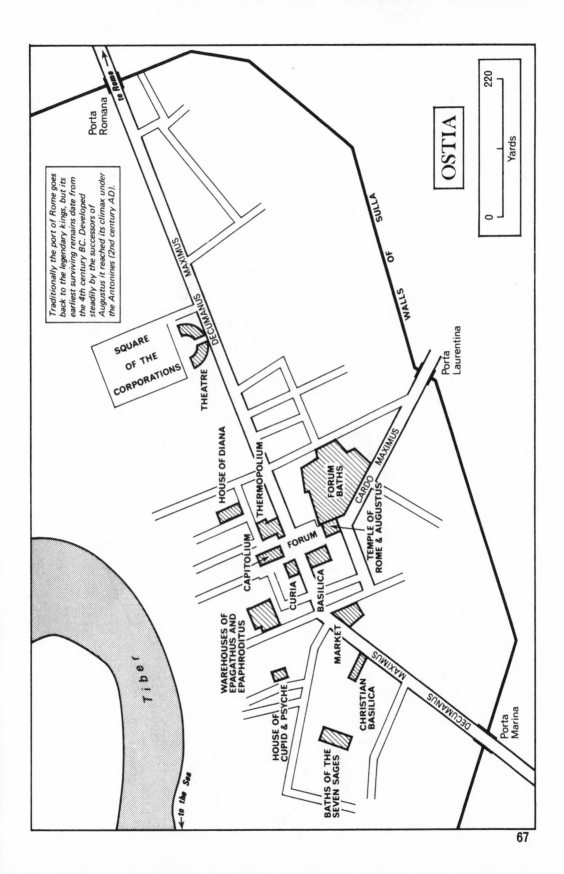

OSTIA

Traditionally the port of Rome goes back to the legendary kings, but its earliest surviving remains date from the 4th century BC. Developed steadily by the successors of Augustus it reached its climax under the Antonines (2nd century AD).

to Rome

Porta Romana

SQUARE OF THE CORPORATIONS

THEATRE

DECUMANUS MAXIMUS

HOUSE OF DIANA

THERMOPOLIUM

CAPITOLIUM

FORUM

CURIA

BASILICA

FORUM BATHS

CARDO MAXIMUS

TEMPLE OF ROME & AUGUSTUS

WALLS OF SULLA

Porta Laurentina

WAREHOUSES OF EPAGATHUS AND EPAPHRODITUS

HOUSE OF CUPID & PSYCHE

MARKET

CHRISTIAN BASILICA

BATHS OF THE SEVEN SAGES

DECUMANUS MAXIMUS

Porta Marina

Tiber

to the Sea

0   220
Yards

67

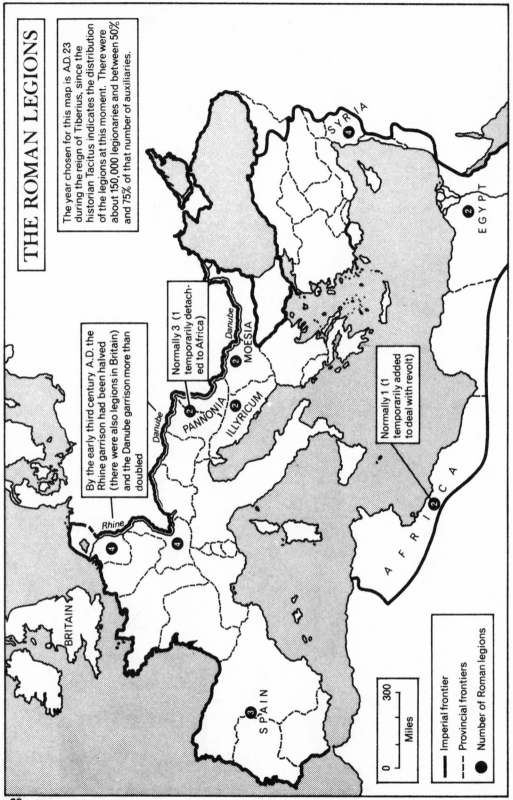

THE ROMAN LEGIONS

The year chosen for this map is A.D.23 during the reign of Tiberius, since the historian Tacitus indicates the distribution of the legions at this moment. There were about 150,000 legionaries and between 50% and 75% of that number of auxiliaries.

By the early third century A.D. the Rhine garrison had been halved (there were also legions in Britain) and the Danube garrison more than doubled

Normally 3 (1 temporarily detached to Africa)

Normally 1 (1 temporarily added to deal with revolt)

SYRIA ④

EGYPT ②

MOESIA ②

PANNONIA ②

ILLYRICUM ②

Danube

Rhine

④ ④

BRITAIN

A F R I C A ②

S P A I N ③

Imperial frontier

Provincial frontiers

● Number of Roman legions

0   300
Miles

68

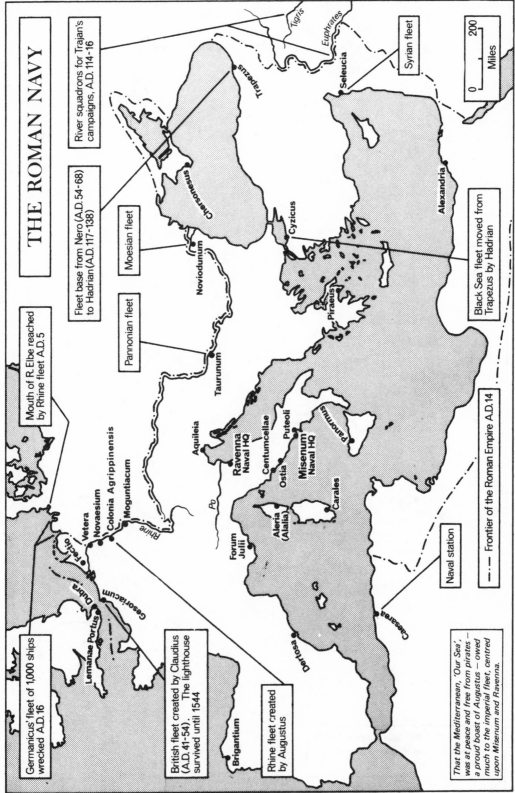

THE ROMAN NAVY

Germanicus' fleet of 1,000 ships wrecked A.D.16

British fleet created by Claudius (A.D.41-54). The lighthouse survived until 1544

Rhine fleet created by Augustus

Mouth of R. Elbe reached by Rhine fleet A.D.5

Fleet base from Nero (A.D. 54-68) to Hadrian (A.D. 117-138)

River squadrons for Trajan's campaigns, A.D. 114-16

Pannonian fleet

Moesian fleet

Syrian fleet

Black Sea fleet moved from Trapezus by Hadrian

Naval station

— ·— Frontier of the Roman Empire A.D.14

That the Mediterranean, 'Our Sea', was at peace and free from pirates — a proud boast of Augustus — owed much to the imperial fleet, centred upon Misenum and Ravenna.

Tigris

Euphrates

Seleucia

Alexandria

Cyzicus

Trapezus

Chersonaesus

Noviodunum

Piraeus

Taurunum

Aquileia

Ravenna Naval HQ

Centumcellae

Ostia

Puteoli

Misenum Naval HQ

Panormus

Carales

Aleria (Alalia)

Po

Forum Julii

Dertosa

Caesarea

Vetera

Novaesium

Colonia Agrippinensis

Moguntiacum

Rhine

Gesoriacum

Portus

Dubris

Lemanae Portus

Brigantium

0   200
Miles

69

BRITANNIA (AD 71)
(AD 59)
(AD 43-47)
Londinium

FREE GERMANY

LOWER GERMANY
Colonia Agrippinensis

Moguntiacum

Rhine

AGRI DECUMAT. (83)

LUGDUNENSIS

UPPER GERMANY

RHAETIA

NORICUM

Danube

PANNONIA

UPPER

LOWER

GALLIA

AQUITANIA

Lugdunum

NARBONENSIS

Nemausus

Aquileia

ILLYRICUM

Adriatic Sea

ITALIA

TARRACONENSIS

HISPANIA

Tarraco

Rome

LUSITANIA

SARDINIA

BAETICA

Corduba

Gades

SICILY

Carthage

MAURETANIA (A.D. 42)

AFRICA

- - - Frontier of Roman Empire A.D. 14
- · - Frontier of Roman Empire A.D. 117
· · · · · Province boundaries

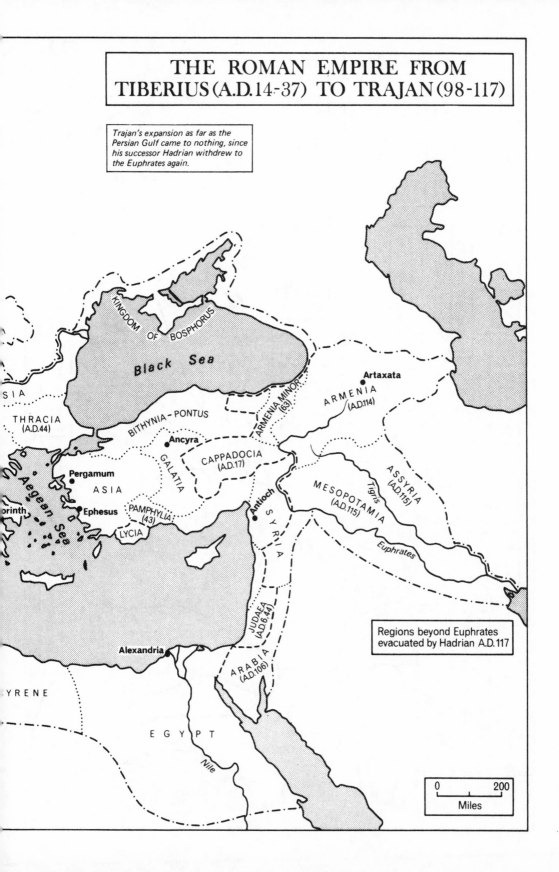

THE ROMAN EMPIRE FROM TIBERIUS (A.D.14-37) TO TRAJAN (98-117)

Trajan's expansion as far as the
Persian Gulf came to nothing, since
his successor Hadrian withdrew to
the Euphrates again.

KINGDOM OF BOSPHORUS

Black Sea

Artaxata

SIA

THRACIA
(A.D.44)

BITHYNIA - PONTUS

ARMENIA MINOR
(63)

ARMENIA
(A.D.114)

Ancyra

Pergamum

GALATIA

CAPPADOCIA
(A.D.17)

ASSYRIA
(A.D.115)

ASIA

Aegean Sea

MESOPOTAMIA
(A.D.115)

Tigris

orinth

Ephesus

PAMPHYLIA
(43)

Antioch

S
Y
R
I
A

LYCIA

Euphrates

JUDAEA
(A.D.6,44)

Regions beyond Euphrates
evacuated by Hadrian A.D.117

Alexandria

ARABIA
(A.D.106)

YRENE

E G Y P T

Nile

0	200

Miles

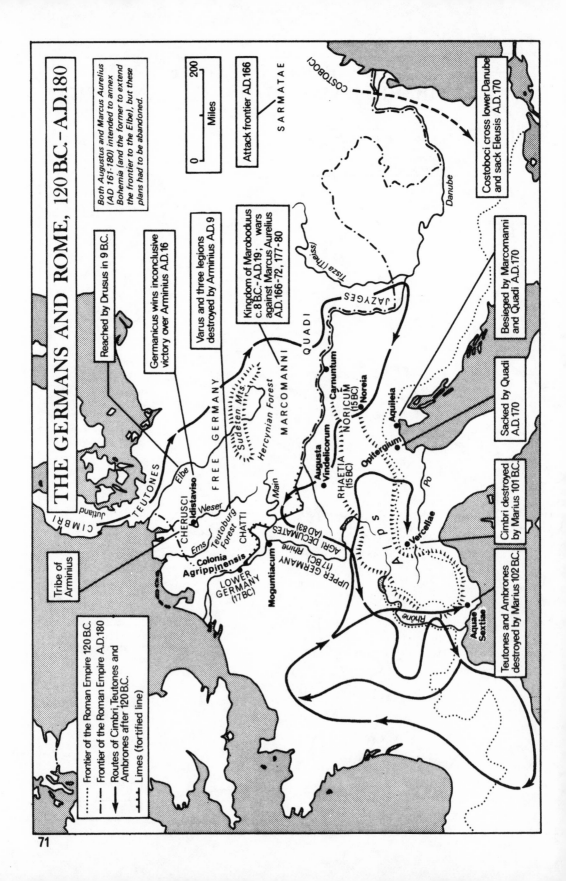

THE GERMANS AND ROME, 120 B.C.–A.D.180

0 — 200 Miles

Both Augustus and Marcus Aurelius (AD 161-180) intended to annex Bohemia (and the former to extend the frontier to the Elbe), but these plans had to be abandoned.

Reached by Drusus in 9 B.C.

Germanicus wins inconclusive victory over Arminius A.D.16

Varus and three legions destroyed by Arminius A.D.9

Kingdom of Maroboduus c.8 B.C.–A.D.19; wars against Marcus Aurelius A.D.166-72, 177-80

Attack frontier A.D.166

Costoboci cross lower Danube and sack Eleusis A.D.170

Besieged by Marcommanni and Quadi A.D.170

Sacked by Quadi A.D.170

Cimbri destroyed by Marius 101 B.C.

Teutones and Ambrones destroyed by Marius 102 B.C.

Tribe of Arminius

SARMATAE

COSTOBOCI

Danube

Tisza (Theiss)

JAZYGES

QUADI

MARCOMANNI

FREE GERMANY

Sudeten Mts.

Hercynian Forest

Elbe

Weser

Ems

Main

CHERUSCI Idistaviso

Teutoburg Forest

CHATTI

Colonia Agrippinensis

Moguntiacum

LOWER GERMANY (17BC)

UPPER GERMANY (17BC)

AGRI DECUMATES (AD 83)

Rhine

Augusta Vindelicorum

RHAETIA (15BC)

NORICUM (15BC)

Carnuntum

Noreia

Aquileia

Opitergium

Po

A L P S

Vercellae

Rhône

Aquae Sextiae

TEUTONES

Jutland

CIMBRI

Frontier of the Roman Empire 120 B.C.
Frontier of the Roman Empire A.D.180
Routes of Cimbri, Teutones and Ambrones after 120 B.C.
Limes (fortified line)

71

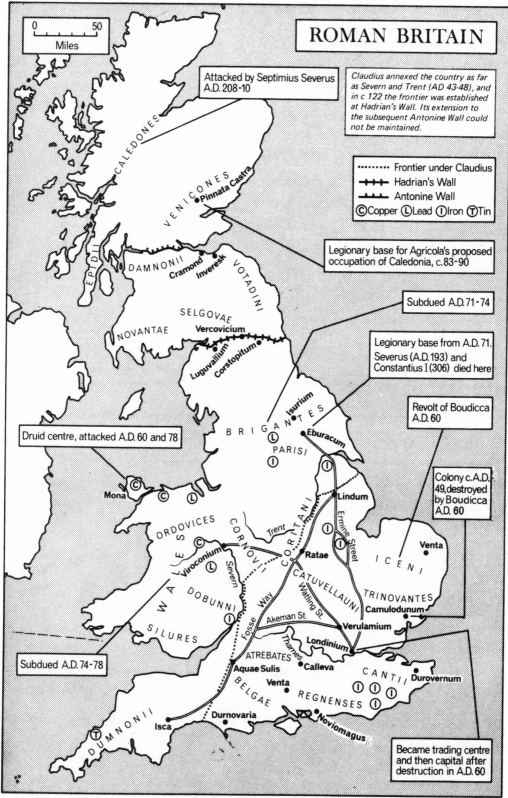

ROMAN BRITAIN

0 — 50 Miles

Attacked by Septimius Severus A.D. 208-10

Claudius annexed the country as far as Severn and Trent (AD 43-48), and in c 122 the frontier was established at Hadrian's Wall. Its extension to the subsequent Antonine Wall could not be maintained.

········· Frontier under Claudius
＋＋＋＋ Hadrian's Wall
━┷━┷━ Antonine Wall
ⒸCopper ⓁLead ⒾIron ⓉTin

CALEDONES

VENICONES

Pinnata Castra

Legionary base for Agricola's proposed occupation of Caledonia, c.83-90

EPIDII

DAMNONII
Cramond Inveresk

VOTADINI

SELGOVAE
Vercovicium

Subdued A.D.71-74

NOVANTAE

Luguvallium Corstopitum

Legionary base from A.D.71. Severus (A.D.193) and Constantius I (306) died here

Isurium
BRIGANTES

Eburacum Ⓛ

Druid centre, attacked A.D. 60 and 78

PARISI Ⓘ

Revolt of Boudicca A.D.60

Mona Ⓒ
Ⓒ Ⓛ

Ⓘ

Lindum

Colony c.A.D. 49, destroyed by Boudicca A.D. 60

ORDOVICES Ⓒ
CORNOVII

Trent

Ⓘ
Ⓘ

Venta

Viroconium Ⓛ

CORITANI

Ratae

ICENI

W A L E S
DOBUNNI

Severn

CATUVELLAUNI

TRINOVANTES

SILURES

Ⓘ

Fosse Way

Watling St.

Camulodunum

Akeman St.

Verulamium

Subdued A.D. 74-78

ATREBATES

Thames

Londinium

Aquae Sulis

Calleva

CANTII

Venta

Durovernum

DUMNONII Ⓣ

BELGAE
Durnovaria

REGNENSES

Ⓘ Ⓘ Ⓘ
Ⓘ

Isca

Noviomagus

Became trading centre and then capital after destruction in A.D.60

72

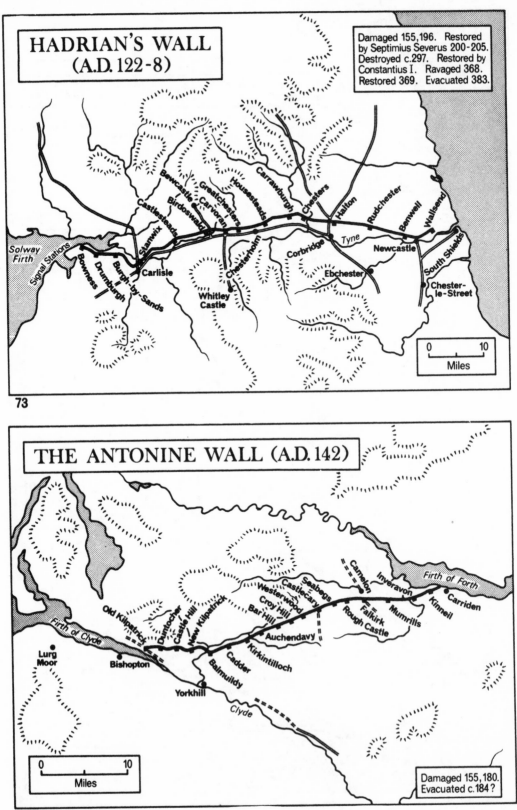

HADRIAN'S WALL
(A.D. 122-8)

Damaged 155, 196. Restored by Septimius Severus 200-205. Destroyed c.297. Restored by Constantius I. Ravaged 368. Restored 369. Evacuated 383.

Solway Firth

Signal Stations

Bowness

Drumburgh

Burgh-by-Sands

Carlisle

Stanwix

Castlesteads

Birdoswald

Bewcastle

Carvoran

Greatchesters

Housesteads

Carrawburgh

Chesters

Halton

Rudchester

Benwell

Wallsend

Newcastle

South Shields

Corbridge

Tyne

Ebchester

Chester-le-Street

Chesterholm

Whitley Castle

0   10
Miles

73

THE ANTONINE WALL (A.D. 142)

Damaged 155, 180. Evacuated c.184?

Firth of Forth

Inveravon

Carriden

Kinneil

Camelon

Mumrills

Falkirk

Rough Castle

Seabegs

Castlecary

Westerwood

Croy Hill

Bar Hill

Auchendavy

Kirkintilloch

Cadder

Balmuildy

Old Kilpatrick

Duntocher

Castle Hill

New Kilpatrick

Firth of Clyde

Lurg Moor

Bishopton

Yorkhill

Clyde

0   10
Miles

74

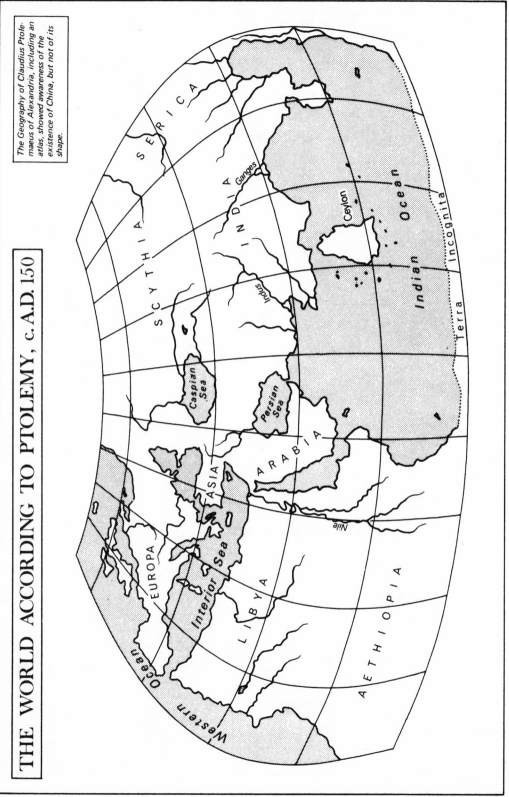

THE WORLD ACCORDING TO PTOLEMY, c. A.D. 150

The Geography of Claudius Ptolemaeus of Alexandria, including an atlas, showed awareness of the existence of China, but not of its shape.

SERICA

SCYTHIA

INDIA

Ganges

Indus

Ceylon

Indian Ocean

Terra Incognita

Caspian Sea

Persian Sea

ARABIA

EUROPA

ASIA

Interior Sea

LIBYA

Nile

AETHIOPIA

Western Ocean

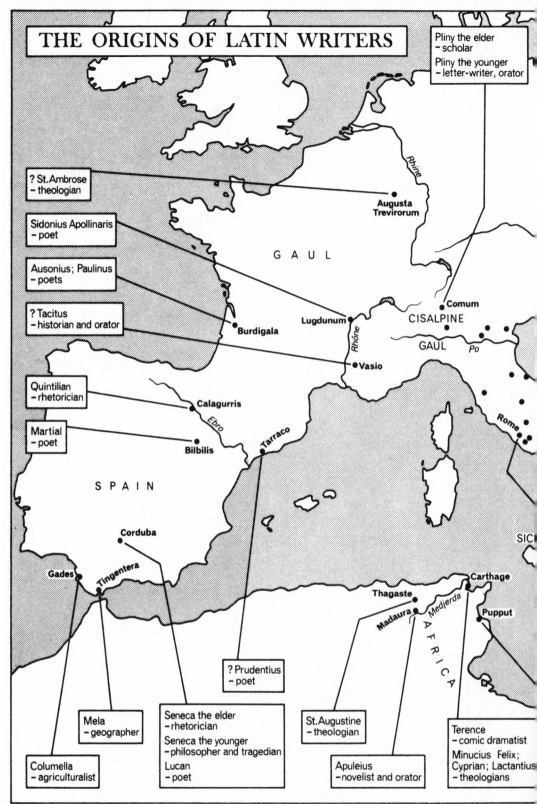

THE ORIGINS OF LATIN WRITERS

Pliny the elder
– scholar
Pliny the younger
– letter-writer, orator

? St.Ambrose
– theologian

Sidonius Apollinaris
– poet

Ausonius; Paulinus
– poets

? Tacitus
– historian and orator

Quintilian
– rhetorician

Martial
– poet

Mela
– geographer

Columella
– agriculturalist

Seneca the elder
– rhetorician
Seneca the younger
– philosopher and tragedian
Lucan
– poet

? Prudentius
– poet

St.Augustine
– theologian

Apuleius
– novelist and orator

Terence
– comic dramatist

Minucius Felix;
Cyprian; Lactantius
– theologians

GAUL

CISALPINE

GAUL

Rhine

Augusta
Trevirorum

Comum

Lugdunum

Rhône

Po

Vasio

Burdigala

Calagurris

Ebro

Tarraco

Bilbilis

Rome

SPAIN

Corduba

Gades

Tingentera

Carthage

Thagaste

Medjerda

Pupput

Madaura

AFRICA

SIC

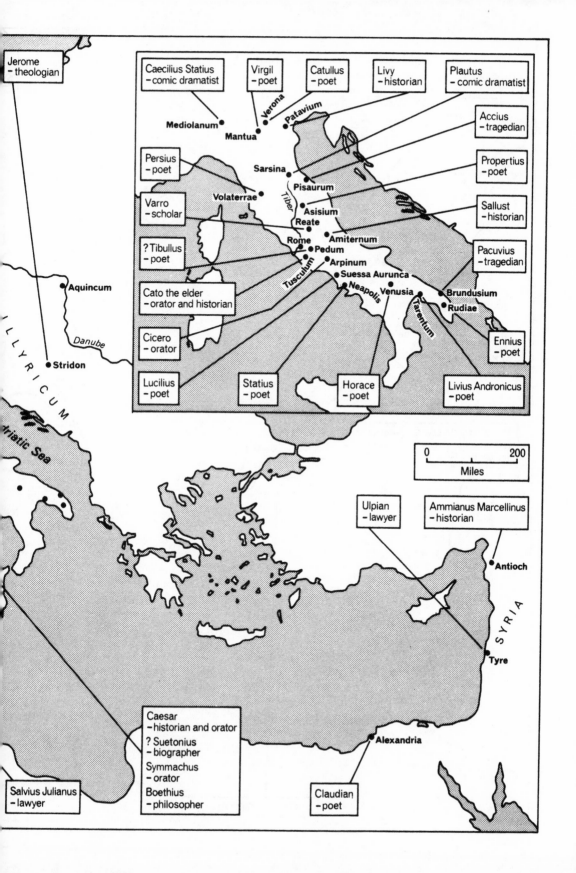

Jerome
– theologian

Caecilius Statius
– comic dramatist

Virgil
– poet

Catullus
– poet

Livy
– historian

Plautus
– comic dramatist

Accius
– tragedian

Persius
– poet

Propertius
– poet

Varro
– scholar

Sallust
– historian

? Tibullus
– poet

Pacuvius
– tragedian

Cato the elder
– orator and historian

Cicero
– orator

Ennius
– poet

Lucilius
– poet

Statius
– poet

Horace
– poet

Livius Andronicus
– poet

Mediolanum

Mantua

Verona

Patavium

Sarsina

Pisaurum

Volaterrae

Tiber

Asisium

Reate

Rome

Amiternum

Pedum

Arpinum

Tusculum

Suessa Aurunca

Neapolis

Venusia

Brundusium

Rudiae

Tarentum

Aquincum

Danube

Stridon

I L L Y R I C U M

Adriatic Sea

0   200
Miles

Ulpian
– lawyer

Ammianus Marcellinus
– historian

Antioch

S Y R I A

Tyre

Alexandria

Caesar
– historian and orator

? Suetonius
– biographer

Symmachus
– orator

Boethius
– philosopher

Salvius Julianus
– lawyer

Claudian
– poet

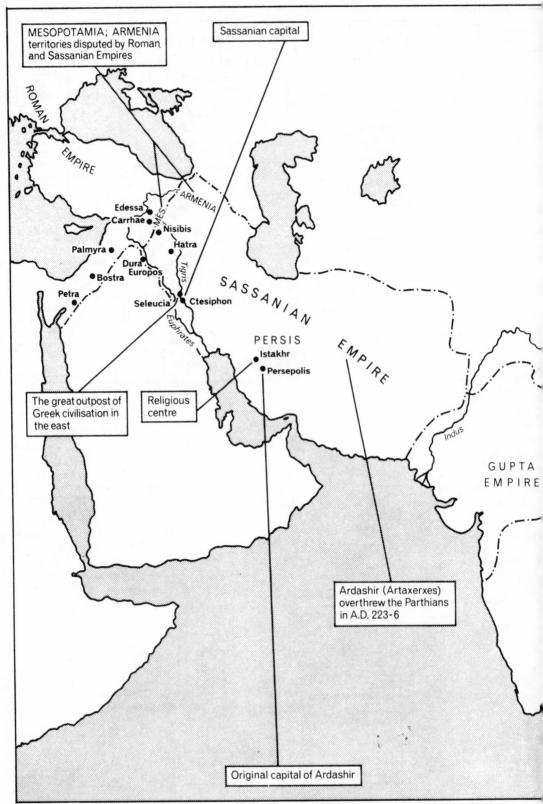

MESOPOTAMIA; ARMENIA territories disputed by Roman and Sassanian Empires

Sassanian capital

ROMAN EMPIRE

ARMENIA

Edessa
Carrhae
Nisibis
MES.
Hatra
Palmyra
Dura Europos
Bostra
Petra
Seleucia
Ctesiphon

Tigris

Euphrates

SASSANIAN

PERSIS
Istakhr
Persepolis

EMPIRE

Indus

GUPTA EMPIRE

The great outpost of Greek civilisation in the east

Religious centre

Ardashir (Artaxerxes) overthrew the Parthians in A.D. 223-6

Original capital of Ardashir

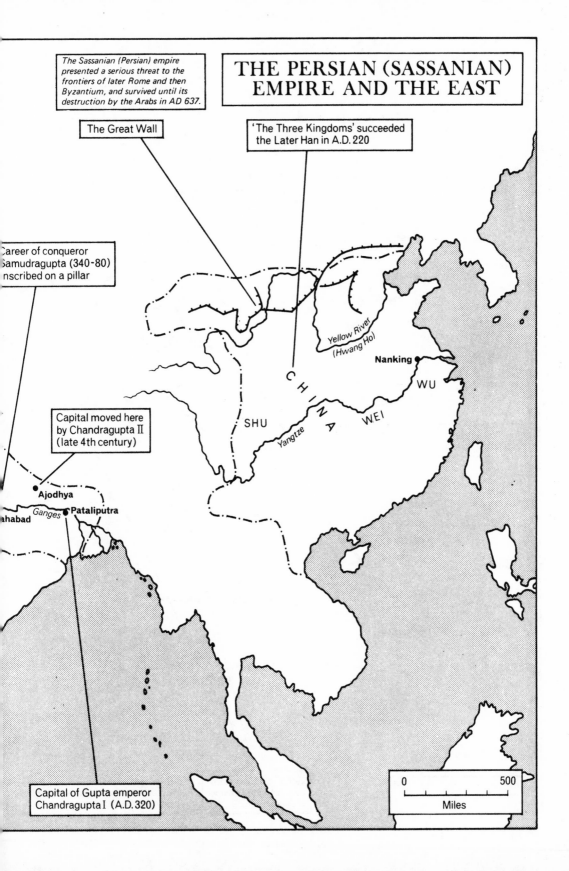

THE PERSIAN (SASSANIAN) EMPIRE AND THE EAST

The Sassanian (Persian) empire presented a serious threat to the frontiers of later Rome and then Byzantium, and survived until its destruction by the Arabs in AD 637.

The Great Wall

'The Three Kingdoms' succeeded the Later Han in A.D. 220

Career of conqueror Samudragupta (340-80) inscribed on a pillar

Capital moved here by Chandragupta II (late 4th century)

Capital of Gupta emperor Chandragupta I (A.D. 320)

Yellow River (Hwang Ho)

Nanking

CHINA

WU

SHU

WEI

Yangtze

Ajodhya

Ganges

Pataliputra

ahabad

0   500

Miles

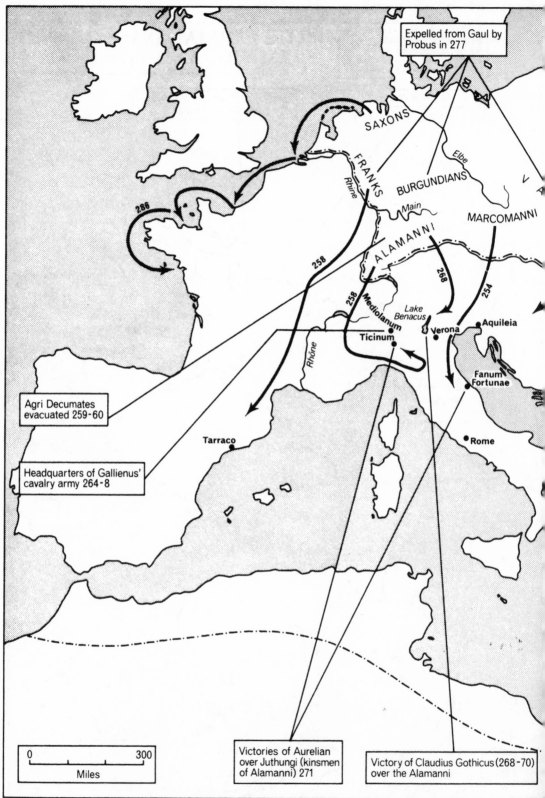

Expelled from Gaul by Probus in 277

SAXONS

FRANKS

Rhine

Elbe

BURGUNDIANS

MARCOMANNI

Main

286

258

ALAMANNI

268

254

258

Mediolanum

Lake Benacus

Verona

Aquileia

Ticinum

Rhône

Fanum Fortunae

Agri Decumates evacuated 259-60

Tarraco

Rome

Headquarters of Gallienus' cavalry army 264-8

0   300

Miles

Victories of Aurelian over Juthungi (kinsmen of Alamanni) 271

Victory of Claudius Gothicus (268-70) over the Alamanni

GERMAN INVASIONS IN THE THIRD CENTURY A.D.

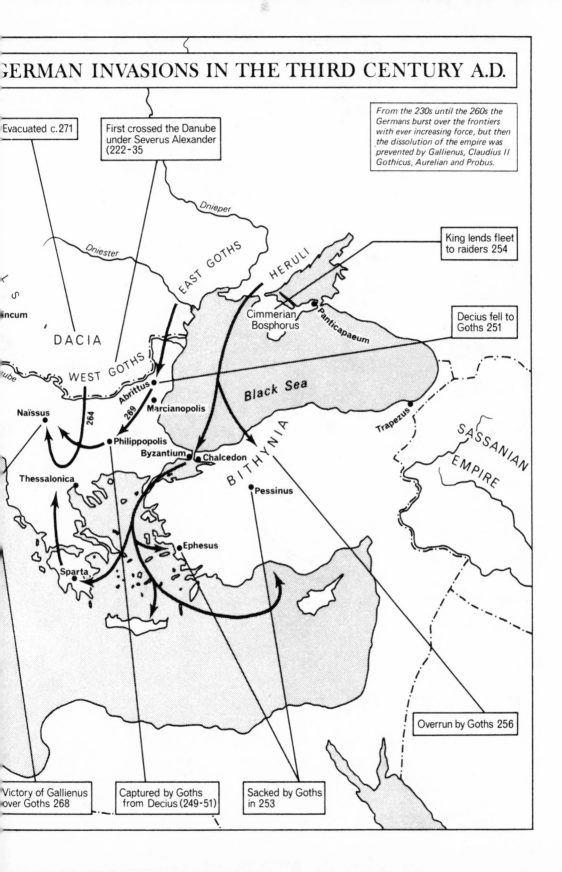

From the 230s until the 260s the Germans burst over the frontiers with ever increasing force, but then the dissolution of the empire was prevented by Gallienus, Claudius II Gothicus, Aurelian and Probus.

Evacuated c.271

First crossed the Danube under Severus Alexander (222-35

King lends fleet to raiders 254

Decius fell to Goths 251

Dnieper

Dniester

EAST GOTHS

HERULI

Cimmerian Bosphorus

Panticapaeum

incum

DACIA

WEST GOTHS

Danube

Abrittus

Naïssus

264

269

Marcianopolis

Black Sea

Trapezus

SASSANIAN EMPIRE

BITHYNIA

Philippopolis

Byzantium

Chalcedon

Thessalonica

Pessinus

Ephesus

Sparta

Overrun by Goths 256

Victory of Gallienus over Goths 268

Captured by Goths from Decius (249-51)

Sacked by Goths in 253

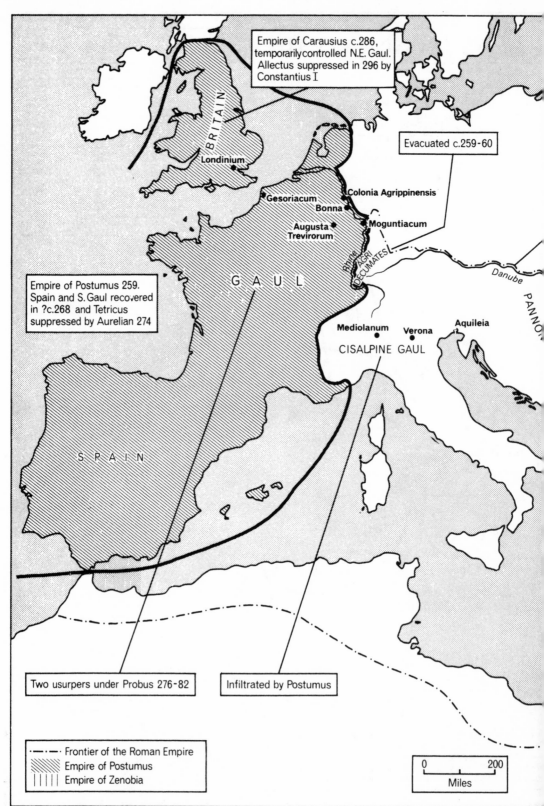

Empire of Carausius c.286, temporarily controlled N.E. Gaul. Allectus suppressed in 296 by Constantius I

Evacuated c.259-60

Empire of Postumus 259. Spain and S. Gaul recovered in ?c.268 and Tetricus suppressed by Aurelian 274

BRITAIN

Londinium

Colonia Agrippinensis

Gesoriacum

Bonna

Augusta Trevirorum

Moguntiacum

G A U L

RHINE

AGRI DECUMATES

Danube

PANNO

Mediolanum • Verona •

Aquileia

CISALPINE GAUL

S P A I N

Two usurpers under Probus 276-82

Infiltrated by Postumus

Frontier of the Roman Empire
Empire of Postumus
Empire of Zenobia

0   200

Miles

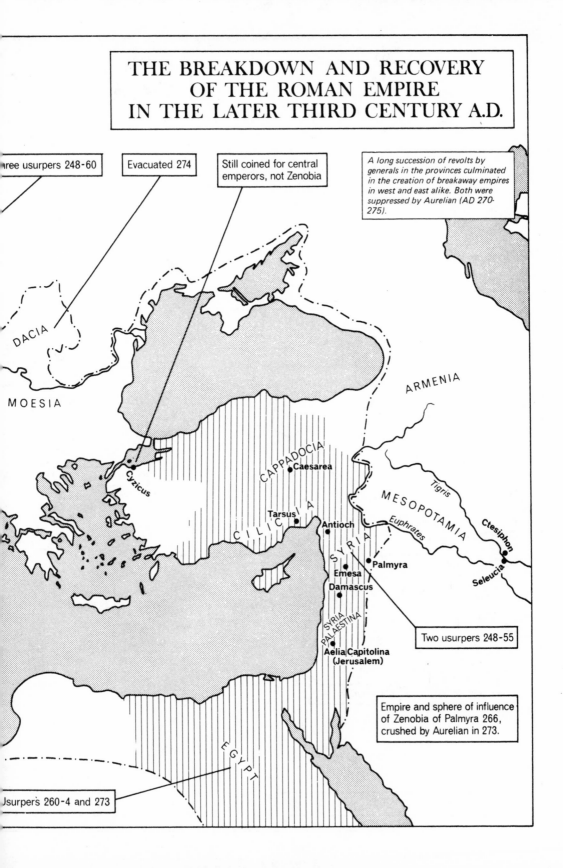

THE BREAKDOWN AND RECOVERY
OF THE ROMAN EMPIRE
IN THE LATER THIRD CENTURY A.D.

ree usurpers 248-60

Evacuated 274

Still coined for central emperors, not Zenobia

A long succession of revolts by generals in the provinces culminated in the creation of breakaway empires in west and east alike. Both were suppressed by Aurelian (AD 270-275).

DACIA

MOESIA

ARMENIA

CAPPADOCIA
Caesarea

Cyzicus

Tigris

MESOPOTAMIA

Ctesiphon

Tarsus
CILICIA
Antioch
Euphrates

S Y R I A

Palmyra

Emesa
Seleucia

Damascus

SYRIA
PALAESTINA

Two usurpers 248-55

Aelia Capitolina
(Jerusalem)

Empire and sphere of influence of Zenobia of Palmyra 266, crushed by Aurelian in 273.

E G Y P T

Usurpers 260-4 and 273

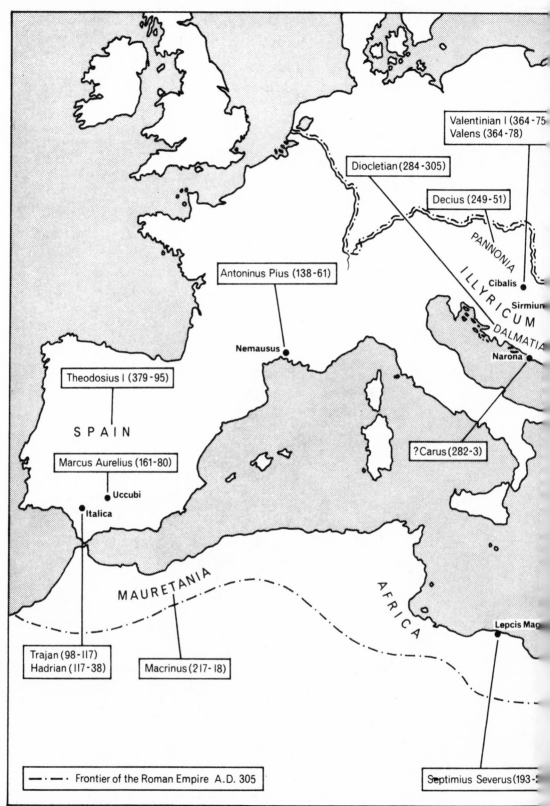

Valentinian I (364-75
Valens (364-78)

Diocletian (284-305)

Decius (249-51)

PANNONIA

ILLYRICUM

Cibalis

Sirmiun

Antoninus Pius (138-61)

DALMATIA

Narona

Nemausus

Theodosius I (379-95)

SPAIN

?Carus (282-3)

Marcus Aurelius (161-80)

Uccubi

Italica

MAURETANIA

AFRICA

Lepcis Mag

Trajan (98-117)
Hadrian (117-38)

Macrinus (217-18)

—·—· Frontier of the Roman Empire A.D. 305

Septimius Severus (193-

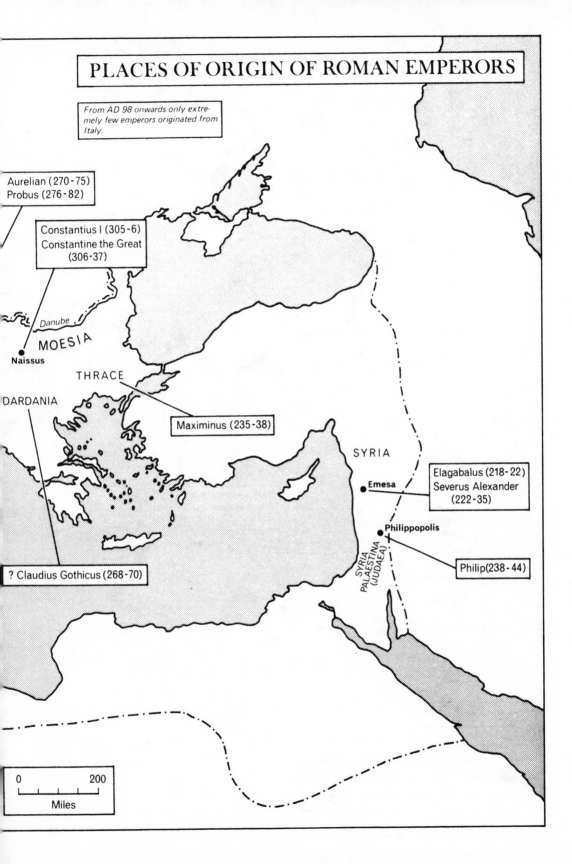

PLACES OF ORIGIN OF ROMAN EMPERORS

From AD 98 onwards only extremely few emperors originated from Italy.

Aurelian (270-75)
Probus (276-82)

Constantius I (305-6)
Constantine the Great
(306-37)

Danube

MOESIA

Naissus

THRACE

DARDANIA

Maximinus (235-38)

SYRIA

Elagabalus (218-22)
Severus Alexander
(222-35)

Emesa

Philippopolis

SYRIA
PALAESTINA
(JUDAEA)

Philip(238-44)

? Claudius Gothicus (268-70)

0   200

Miles

Colonia

GERMANIA

Rhine

Regina

Aquincum

PANNONIA

Mursa

Lutetia

Genabum

Vesontio

Alps

Tergeste

Ravenna

DALMATIA

GAUL

Genua

ITALY

Burdigala

APULIA

Tolosa

Pyrenees

Massilia

Rome

CALAB

CAMPANIA

SPAIN

SARDINIA

Jews deported from
Rome by Tiberius
A.D. 14 - 37

Caralis

Panormus

SICILY

Corduba

Gades

Carthage

Melita

Volubilis

Atlas   Mountains

S A H A R A

Oea

0   250

Miles

■ Areas of widespread Jewish settlement

● Towns with large Jewish communities

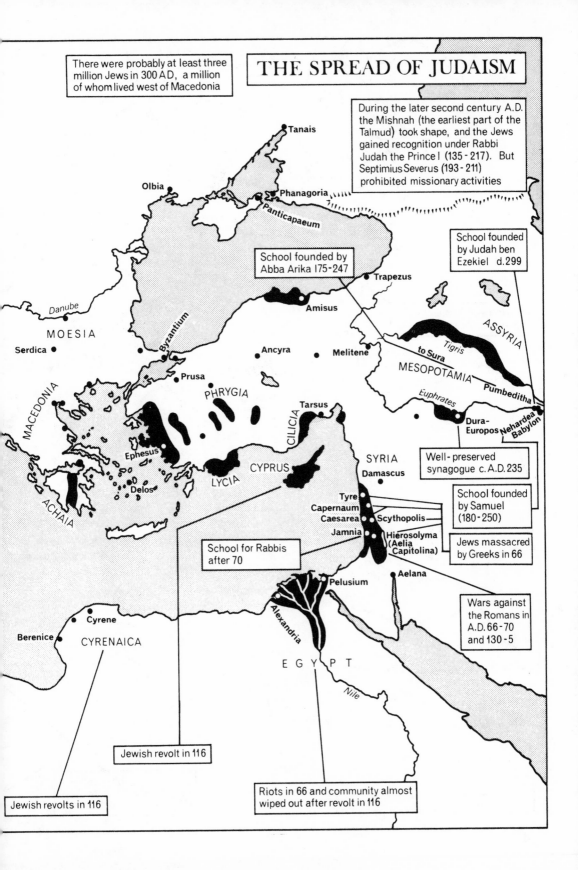

THE SPREAD OF JUDAISM

There were probably at least three million Jews in 300 A.D., a million of whom lived west of Macedonia

During the later second century A.D. the Mishnah (the earliest part of the Talmud) took shape, and the Jews gained recognition under Rabbi Judah the Prince I (135 - 217). But Septimius Severus (193 - 211) prohibited missionary activities

School founded by Judah ben Ezekiel d.299

School founded by Abba Arika 175-247

Tanais

Olbia

Phanagoria

Panticapaeum

Trapezus

Amisus

ASSYRIA

Danube

MOESIA

Serdica ●

Byzantium

Ancyra

Melitene

to Sura

MESOPOTAMIA

Tigris

Pumbeditha

Euphrates

Prusa

PHRYGIA

Tarsus

CILICIA

Dura-
Europos

Nehardea
Babylon

MACEDONIA

Ephesus

CYPRUS

SYRIA

Damascus

Well- preserved synagogue c. A.D. 235

Delos

LYCIA

Tyre

Capernaum

Caesarea

Scythopolis

School founded by Samuel (180 - 250)

ACHAIA

Jamnia

Hierosolyma (Aelia Capitolina)

Jews massacred by Greeks in 66

School for Rabbis after 70

Pelusium

Aelana

Cyrene

Alexandria

Berenice

CYRENAICA

E G Y P T

Wars against the Romans in A.D. 66 - 70 and 130 - 5

Nile

Jewish revolt in 116

Jewish revolts in 116

Riots in 66 and community almost wiped out after revolt in 116

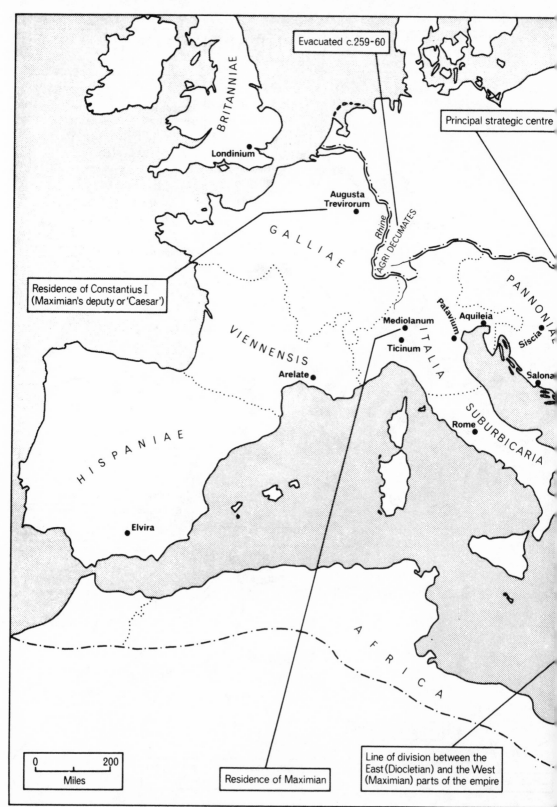

Evacuated c.259-60

Principal strategic centre

BRITANNIAE

Londinium

Augusta
Trevirorum

GALLIAE

Rhine

(AGRI DECUMATES)

Residence of Constantius I
(Maximian's deputy or 'Caesar')

VIENNENSIS

PANNONIA

Mediolanum

Patavium

Aquileia

Siscia

Ticinum

ITALIA

Arelate

Salona

HISPANIAE

SUBURBICARIA

Rome

Elvira

AFRICA

0   200
Miles

Residence of Maximian

Line of division between the
East (Diocletian) and the West
(Maximian) parts of the empire

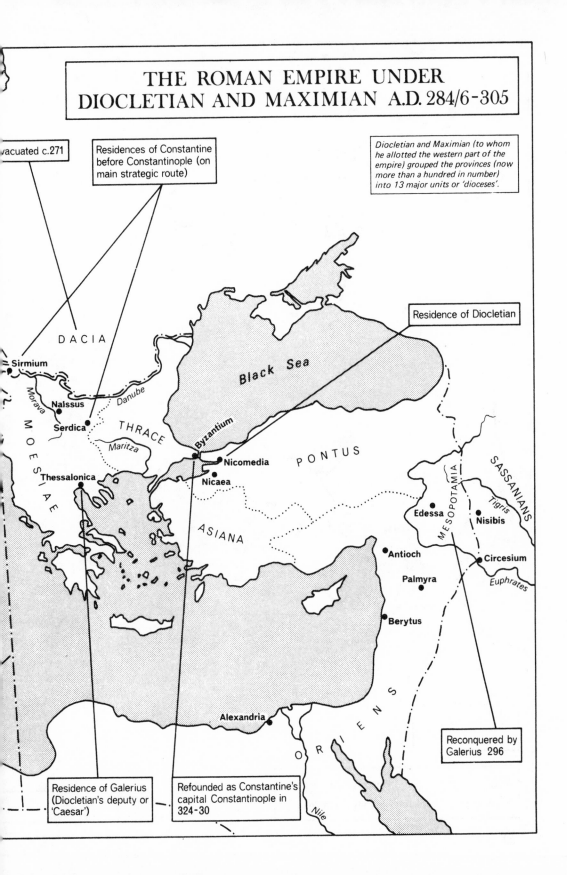

THE ROMAN EMPIRE UNDER DIOCLETIAN AND MAXIMIAN A.D. 284/6-305

vacuated c.271

Residences of Constantine before Constantinople (on main strategic route)

Diocletian and Maximian (to whom he allotted the western part of the empire) grouped the provinces (now more than a hundred in number) into 13 major units or 'dioceses'.

Residence of Diocletian

DACIA

Sirmium

Black Sea

Morava

Danube

Naissus

Serdica

THRACE

Byzantium

Maritza

PONTUS

M O E S I A E

Thessalonica

Nicomedia

Nicaea

SASSANIANS

Tigris

ASIANA

Edessa

MESOPOTAMIA

Nisibis

Antioch

Circesium

Palmyra

Euphrates

Berytus

O R I E N S

Alexandria

Reconquered by Galerius 296

Residence of Galerius (Diocletian's deputy or 'Caesar')

Refounded as Constantine's capital Constantinople in 324-30

Nile

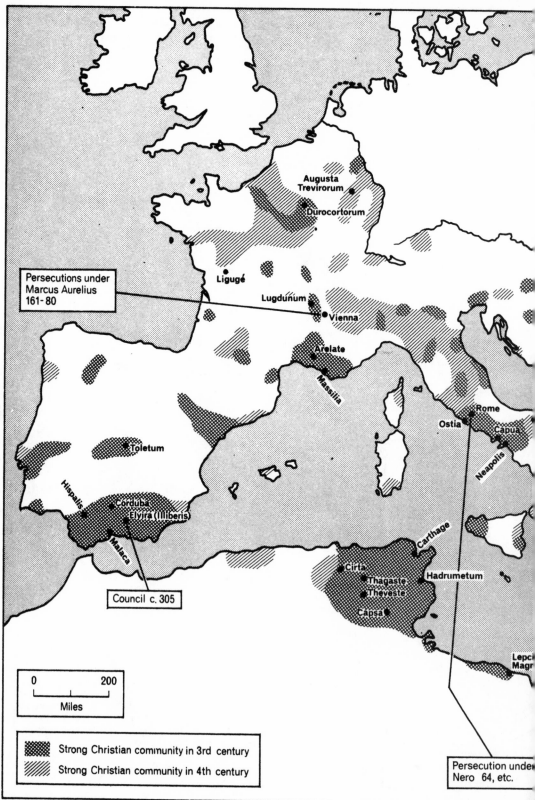

Persecutions under
Marcus Aurelius
161- 80

Augusta
Trevirorum

Durocortorum

Ligugé

Lugdúnum

Vienna

Arelate

Massilia

Rome

Ostia

Capua

Neapolis

Toletum

Hispalis

Corduba
Elvira (Illiberis)

Malaca

Carthage

Cirta

Thagaste

Theveste

Hadrumetum

Capsa

Lepci
Magr

Council c. 305

0   200

Miles

Strong Christian community in 3rd century

Strong Christian community in 4th century

Persecution under
Nero 64, etc.

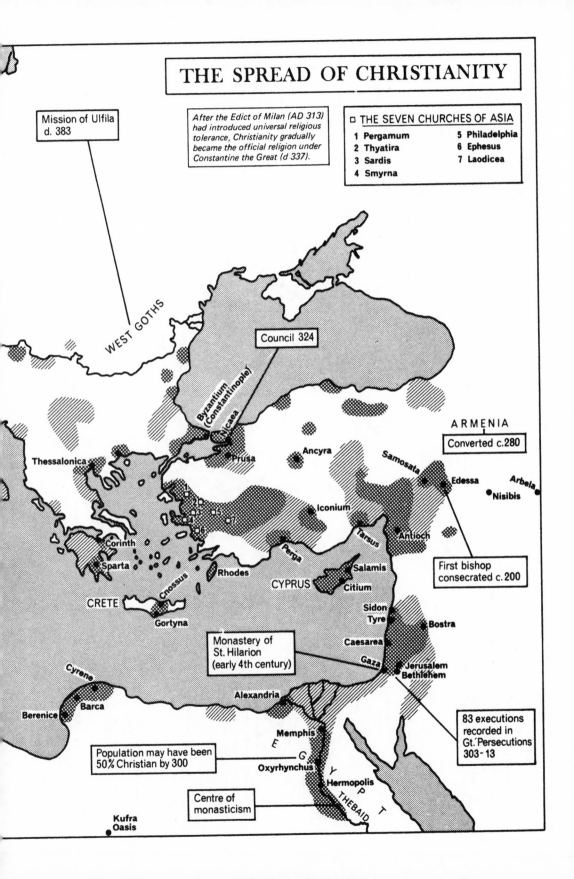

THE SPREAD OF CHRISTIANITY

Mission of Ulfila
d. 383

*After the Edict of Milan (AD 313)
had introduced universal religious
tolerance, Christianity gradually
became the official religion under
Constantine the Great (d 337).*

☐ THE SEVEN CHURCHES OF ASIA

1 Pergamum   5 Philadelphia
2 Thyatira   6 Ephesus
3 Sardis   7 Laodicea
4 Smyrna

WEST GOTHS

Council 324

Byzantium
(Constantinople)
Nicaea

ARMENIA
Converted c.280

Thessalonica

Prusa

Ancyra

Samosata

Edessa

Arbela

Nisibis

Iconium

Tarsus

Antioch

Corinth

Perga

First bishop
consecrated c.200

Sparta

Rhodes

CRETE

Cnossus

Salamis

CYPRUS

Citium

Sidon

Tyre

Bostra

Gortyna

Caesarea

Monastery of
St. Hilarion
(early 4th century)

Gaza

Jerusalem
Bethlehem

Cyrene

Barca

Berenice

Alexandria

83 executions
recorded in
Gt. Persecutions
303 - 13

Memphis

E
G
Y
P
T

Population may have been
50% Christian by 300

Oxyrhynchus

Hermopolis

THEBAID

Centre of
monasticism

Kufra
Oasis

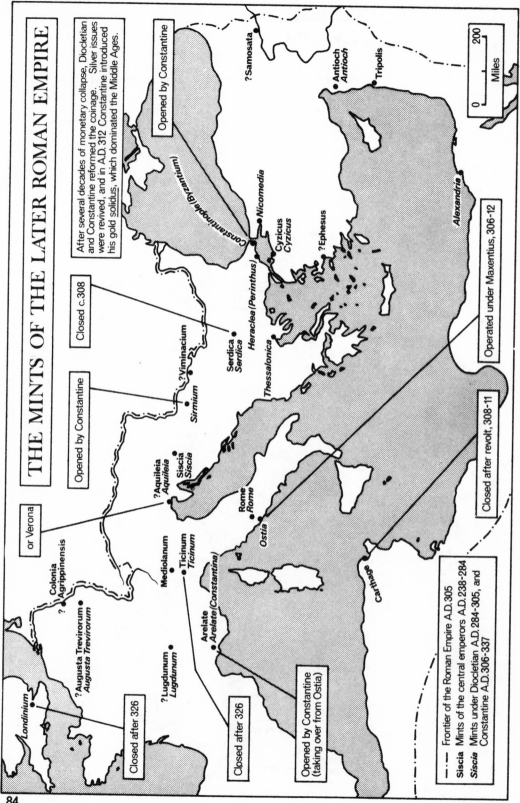

THE MINTS OF THE LATER ROMAN EMPIRE

After several decades of monetary collapse, Diocletian and Constantine reformed the coinage. Silver issues were revived, and in A.D. 312 Constantine introduced his gold solidus, which dominated the Middle Ages.

Opened by Constantine

Closed c.308

Opened by Constantine

or Verona

Closed after 326

Closed after 326

Opened by Constantine (taking over from Ostia)

Operated under Maxentius, 306-12

Closed after revolt, 308-11

?Samosata

Antioch
Antioch

Tripolis

Nicomedia

Cyzicus
Cyzicus

?Ephesus

Constantinople *(Byzantium)*

Alexandria

Heraclea (Perinthus)

Serdica
Serdica

?Viminacium

Sirmium

Thessalonica

?Aquileia
Aquileia

Siscia
Siscia

Rome
Rome

Ostia

Mediolanum

Ticinum
Ticinum

Arelate (Constantina)
Arelate (Constantina)

Colonia
Agrippinensis
?

?Augusta Trevirorum
Augusta Trevirorum

?Lugdunum
Lugdunum

Londinium

Carthage

— · — Frontier of the Roman Empire A.D. 305

Siscia Mints of the central emperors A.D. 238-284

Siscia Mints under Diocletian A.D. 284-305, and Constantine A.D. 306-337

0   200
Miles

84

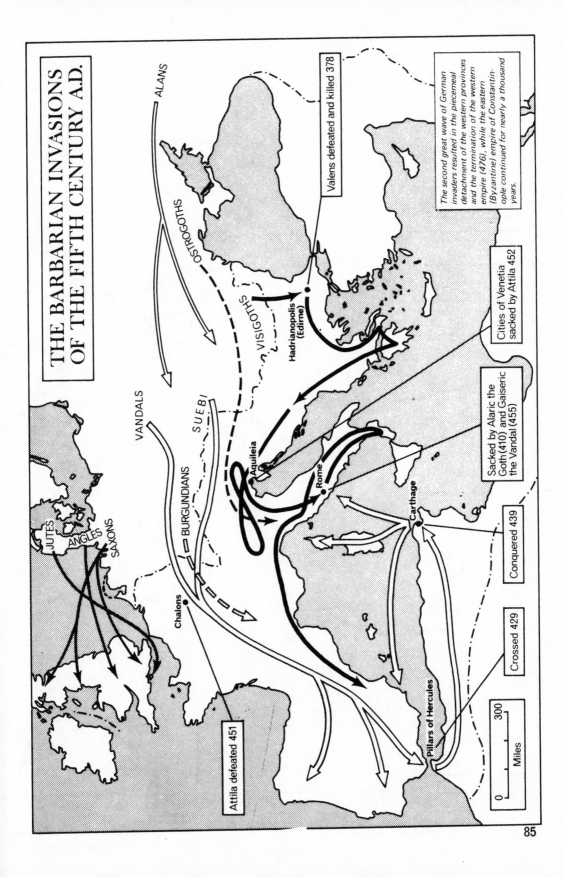

THE BARBARIAN INVASIONS OF THE FIFTH CENTURY A.D.

ALANS

OSTROGOTHS

VISIGOTHS

VANDALS

SUEBI

BURGUNDIANS

JUTES

ANGLES

SAXONS

Chalons

Aquileia

Rome

Carthage

Hadrianopolis (Edirne)

Pillars of Hercules

Valens defeated and killed 378

The second great wave of German invaders resulted in the piecemeal detachment of the western provinces and the termination of the western empire (476), while the eastern (Byzantine) empire of Constantinople continued for nearly a thousand years.

Cities of Venetia sacked by Attila 452

Sacked by Alaric the Goth (410) and Gaiseric the Vandal (455)

Conquered 439

Crossed 429

Attila defeated 451

0   300

Miles

85

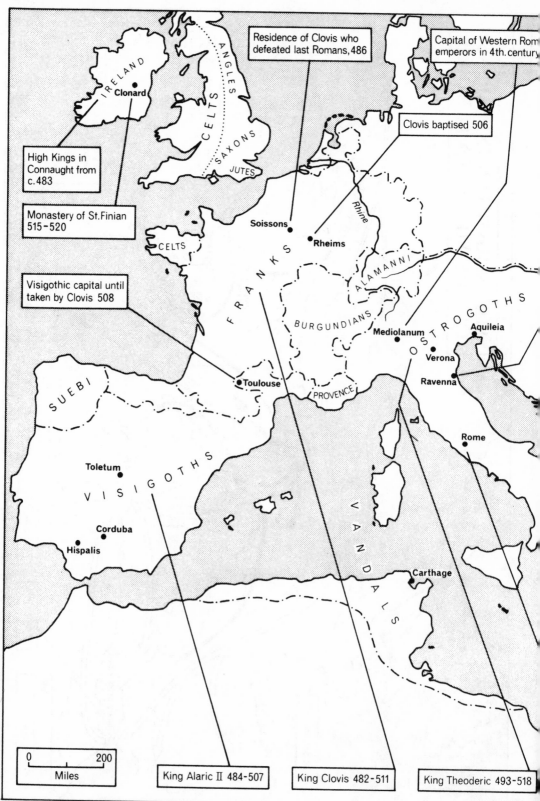

Residence of Clovis who defeated last Romans, 486

Capital of Western Rom[an] emperors in 4th. century

Clovis baptised 506

High Kings in Connaught from c.483

Monastery of St.Finian 515-520

Visigothic capital until taken by Clovis 508

IRELAND

Clonard

ANGLES

CELTS

SAXONS

JUTES

CELTS

Rhine

FRANKS

Soissons

Rheims

ALAMANNI

BURGUNDIANS

OSTROGOTHS

Mediolanum

Aquileia

Verona

Ravenna

SUEBI

Toulouse

PROVENCE

Rome

Toletum

VISIGOTHS

VANDALS

Corduba

Hispalis

Carthage

0	200

Miles

King Alaric II 484-507

King Clovis 482-511

King Theoderic 493-518

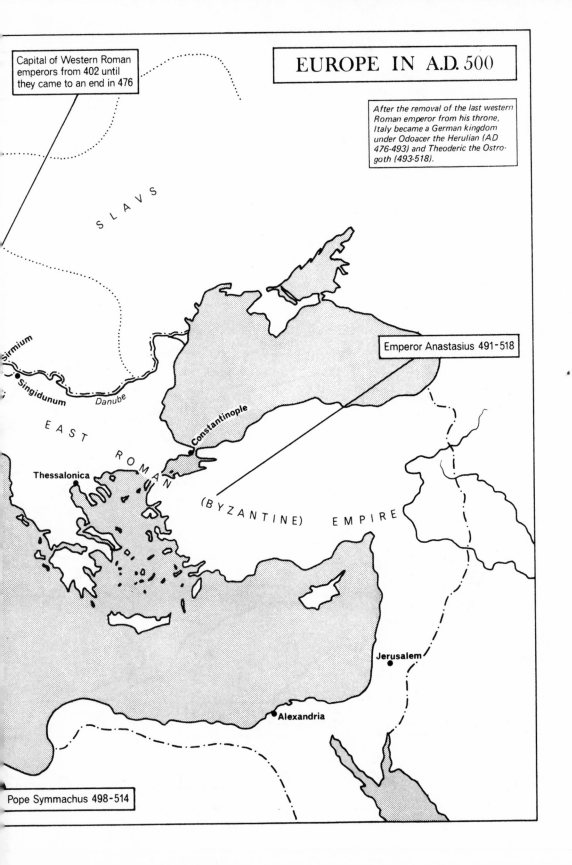

EUROPE IN A.D. 500

Capital of Western Roman emperors from 402 until they came to an end in 476

After the removal of the last western Roman emperor from his throne, Italy became a German kingdom under Odoacer the Herulian (AD 476-493) and Theoderic the Ostrogoth (493-518).

SLAVS

Sirmium

Singidunum   Danube

Emperor Anastasius 491-518

EAST

ROMAN

Constantinople

Thessalonica

(BYZANTINE) EMPIRE

Jerusalem

Alexandria

Pope Symmachus 498-514

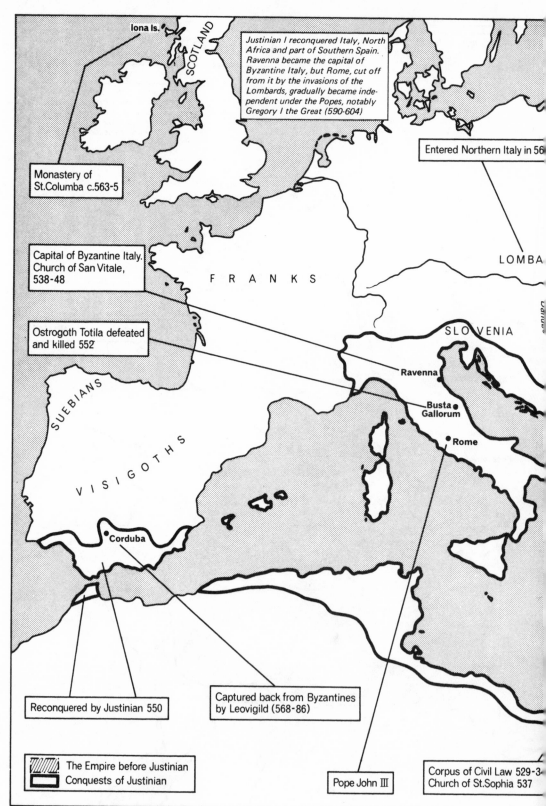

Iona Is.

SCOTLAND

Justinian I reconquered Italy, North
Africa and part of Southern Spain.
Ravenna became the capital of
Byzantine Italy, but Rome, cut off
from it by the invasions of the
Lombards, gradually became inde-
pendent under the Popes, notably
Gregory I the Great (590-604)

Entered Northern Italy in 56

Monastery of
St.Columba c.563-5

LOMBA

FRANKS

SLOVENIA

Capital of Byzantine Italy.
Church of San Vitale,
538-48

Ostrogoth Totila defeated
and killed 552

Ravenna

SUEBIANS

Busta
Gallorum

Rome

VISIGOTHS

Corduba

Reconquered by Justinian 550

Captured back from Byzantines
by Leovigild (568-86)

The Empire before Justinian
Conquests of Justinian

Pope John III

Corpus of Civil Law 529-3
Church of St.Sophia 537

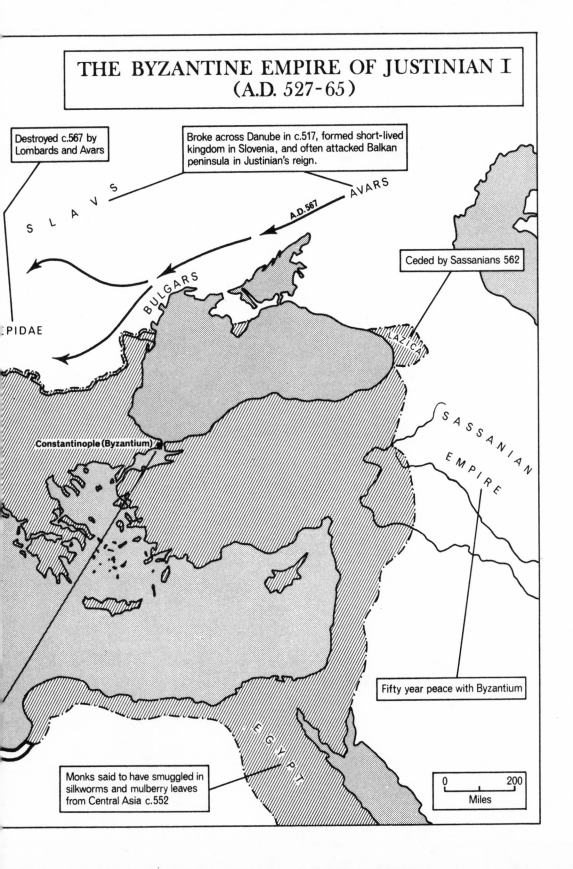

THE BYZANTINE EMPIRE OF JUSTINIAN I
(A.D. 527-65)

Destroyed c.567 by Lombards and Avars

Broke across Danube in c.517, formed short-lived kingdom in Slovenia, and often attacked Balkan peninsula in Justinian's reign.

Ceded by Sassanians 562

S L A V S

AVARS

A.D. 567

BULGARS

:PIDAE

LAZICA

Constantinople (Byzantium)

S A S S A N I A N

E M P I R E

Fifty year peace with Byzantium

E G Y P T

Monks said to have smuggled in silkworms and mulberry leaves from Central Asia c.552

0   200
Miles

Index of Place Names[1]

Modern names are given in brackets

[1] I have sometimes sacrificed consistency of spelling to convenience and tradition.